Community Education, Learning and Development

THIRD EDITION

Lyn Tett

Professor of Community Education and Lifelong Learning at
the Moray House School of Education, University of Edinburgh

with a chapter by
Ian Fyfe

Lecturer, Department of Higher and Community Education at
the Moray House School of Education, University of Edinburgh

Published by
Dunedin Academic Press Ltd
Hudson House
8 Albany Street
Edinburgh EH1 3QB
Scotland

Third Edition 2010
First Published 2002 as
Community Education, Lifelong Learning and Social Inclusion
Second Impression 2003
Second Edition 2006

ISBN 978-1-906716-10-3
ISSN 1479–6910

British Library Cataloguing in Publication data
A catalogue record for this book is available from the British Library

Typeset by Makar Publishing Production, Edinburgh
Printed and bound by CPI Group (UK) Ltd, Croydon, CR0 4YY

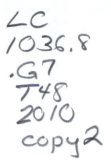
Dedication

This book is dedicated both to the memory of my parents, Eric and Violet Dowse, with thanks for all the sacrifices they made to support my generation and also to my grandchildren, Dominic, Kieran, Scarlett, Lulu and Angus with the hope that they will be able to experience a more socially just world.

Contents

Acknowledgements

I would like to thank Paul Tett and Jim Crowther for commenting on some of the chapters and so enabling me to improve them. I am also grateful to colleagues and students in community education as well as friends and family for supporting me through the writing of this book.

Introduction

The overall aim of this book is to analyse the conceptual, policy and political ideas underpinning community education and the varieties of practice in which community educators engage. Community education's primary purpose is education within and for communities. However, it can be difficult to define as its focus varies over time in response to changing local, national and global educational priorities, so the first chapter begins with a discussion of the traditions that have underpinned current practices. It traces the social and economic developments in the nineteenth century that led to demands for social reforms and argues that the practice that followed represented two main traditions that either challenged or supported the status quo and shows that these traditions are still present in policy and practice today. The first chapter also discusses another factor that impacts on the work of community educators—the ways in which the notion of 'community' is defined. It argues that the concept of community has been used in policy and practice to create boundaries around what counts as acceptable action for community educators for example, when a community is seen as only comprising people living in particular geographical areas. It then goes on to discuss how solidarities across the different types of communities— of place, interest and function—can be developed.

The second chapter explores in detail how community education has developed in Scotland through an examination of the assumptions behind government policies and the ensuing practice developments. The focus is on the spaces that these policies create for making a real difference to the lives of people. Chapter 3 also focuses on policy discourses. It traces the rise of lifelong learning up the policy agenda, identifies the underlying assumptions that are made and the implications of these for community educators. It argues that whilst a commitment to lifelong learning brings many opportunities for growth, development and fulfilment, without careful intervention within a social justice framework, it can also serve to reinforce inequalities.

The next three chapters focus on the ways in which practice can create spaces that challenge narrow policy conceptualisations and a number of community education, learning and development projects are examined. This wide variety of practice is chosen to make a case for a model of learning that focuses on greater participation in democratic decision-making by everyone. The practice contexts include: family literacy and health education (Chapter 4); young people and community engagement (Chapter 5—written by Ian Fyfe); partnerships, community capacity building and active citizenship (Chapter 6). This latter chapter also examines whether community education can make a difference to people's lives through challenging dominant discourses that position people as victims who need to have 'experts' show them what to do. It describes strategies that can encourage people to take back control so that the ability of all citizens can be acknowledged and people can define their own problems and find appropriate solutions.

Finally, the argument is made that community educators, and those concerned with learning and development, have an important but difficult role to fulfil. They need to recognise competing interests whilst also seeking to build mutual understandings and cooperation in ways that enable the voices of those that are excluded to be heard. It is suggested that the challenge for community education is to support the type of learning and development that leads to social justice for everyone through the development of imaginative and transgressive solutions to seemingly intractable difficulties.

Chapter 1

Community Education: Antecedents and Meanings

> Education for the labouring poor would be prejudicial to their morals and happiness; it would teach them to despise their lot in life instead of making them good servants in agriculture and other laborious employments.
> (Hansard 1st series, ix, 1807: cols 798–9)

Introduction

Community education's primary purpose is education *within* and *for* communities. This involves a blurring of traditional boundaries and an emphasis on education that grows out of people's experiences and the social interests that are generated within communities. It has a different focus from mainstream education both in its curriculum and in its methods. Community education is about encouraging and engaging people throughout life into learning that is based on what they are interested in. Education is developed that is relevant to the participating learners and is responsive to community priorities identified *with* people rather than *for* them. The motivation and purpose for learning by the participants will change over time, but if education is rooted in communities 'it will allow genuinely alternative and democratic agendas to emerge at the local level' (Martin, 1996:140).

Although it is one of the newer forms of educational development, compared to formal educational institutions such as schools, the conceptual origins of community education stem from two much older traditions. These originated in the early nineteenth century when rapid economic growth and industrial development led to the first demands for social reforms (see Crowther, 1999; Shaw, 2003). One of these traditions came from the radical working class organisations that developed popular educational activities through existing networks of support and solidarity. This involved acting and educating against the status quo in order to develop 'knowledge calculated to make you free' (Johnson, 1988).

The other tradition is derived from the philanthropic provision of education in communities for poor, working-class adults and young people, largely organised by Christian socialist bodies, in order to help alleviate 'problems, strengthen character, encourage independence and preserve the family' (Shaw, 2003:10).

Community education can be difficult to define as its focus varies over time in response to changing local, national and global educational priorities. So in trying to locate it both historically and contextually two issues have to be addressed. One is that 'community' is an ambivalent concept that is difficult to define but, as Raymond Williams noted, 'never seems to be used unfavourably' (1976: 66). The other is that community education activities include a very wide range of educational practices that come from different traditions with a range of purposes, meanings and intentions. These traditions are also influenced by the ways in which the nation state attempts to adapt educational policy and practice to changing ideologies and social and economic conditions. As the opening quotation of this chapter demonstrates, education for 'the labouring poor' has long been a source of contention and the different ideologies underpinning these disputes are brought into focus by the lens of community education.

In this chapter the antecedents of community education will first be explored and then attention will turn to discussing what is meant by the concept of 'community' and how its different interpretations are reflected in both formal definitions of education policy and the informal politics of local practice.

Antecedents of community education

Community education has grown out of organisations that have regarded their primary purpose as involving young people and adults in a range of activities. In this section the historical roots of those organisations that have emphasised educational work in communities are explored in order to identify both the underpinning ideas and the types of practice advocated. The focus will be on the extent to which the purposes of these organisations have identified local development, mutual support and social action as the key components of the education process.

Involving young people

Work directed at working-class young people first developed in the nineteenth century out of concerns about the deteriorating economic conditions that were impacting on those that had moved to the cities in search of employment. The squalid conditions in which poor young people were living were thought by the more affluent members of society to be affecting the potential for intellectual and emotional development of this group (Smith, 1988). The solution proposed was to give young people opportunities outside of these environments in order to improve their character and sense of responsibility (Smith, 1988). Youth work organisations began to develop and grow in the 1860s, particularly in London where the differences between rich and poor were most starkly contrasted and visible to the growing middle classes (Malone, 2002). George Williams founded the first organisation, the Young Men's Christian Association (YMCA), in 1844 in London. Provision was underpinned by Christian Socialist principles and was dedicated to replacing young men's life on the streets with prayer and Bible study (Smith, 1988). The YMCA was quickly followed by many other organisations that had similar intentions and the work was developed mainly by different Christian Churches.

The sponsors of youth work provision felt that the best way to attract young people was to provide facilities where they could enjoy themselves, but in return for this opportunity they would have to submit to being improved. As Mark Smith argued:

> Sponsors of early clubs and youth provision recognised that if they were to safeguard the values and institutions that they believed in then young people would have to be socialised into seeing the world as they did. (Smith, 1988: 13)

This led to much youth work, particularly that targeted at boys, as having three main objectives: recreation, education, religion. Recreation was what attracted people into the clubs, education included physical, moral and mental training and religion comprised 'all the impalpable influences which give a club a grip on its members and tend to awaken their higher nature' (Russell and Rigby, 1908: 20). Work that focused on girls and young women placed more of an emphasis on relationships and gentle improvement so that girls might 'ennoble the class to which they belong' (Stanley, 1890: 48) and positively influence the men in their lives. Others argued, however, that the conditions in which girls worked also needed to be addressed and set out to improve these environmental issues through intervention in the public and private domains of girls' lives (Spence, 1999). For example, Lily Montagu (1904: 250), who was one of the founders of the National Organisation of Girls Clubs, suggested that 'if girls work for less than a living wage, in a vitiated atmosphere, they are not likely to become the strong, self controlled women whom we desire the clubs to train'.

Many of the distinctively bourgeois values on which youth work was based were dawn from the experience of their sponsors of public schooling and military service or represented ideal paradigms of middle-class leisure. The positive virtues derived from these experiences were contrasted with working-class culture that was seen as overly focused on the excitement that came from the theatres of the time and too self-centred and inward looking (Blanch, 1979). Youth work's focus from this perspective was to direct working-class leisure into respectable channels, with either a religious or military bias or both. In addition, a number of youth work organisations, especially the uniformed groups such as the Boys' Brigade, Scouts and Guides (founded in the late nineteenth and early twentieth centuries) had explicitly colonial and conservative values and aims where boys were 'prepared for war or the workplace and girls to be housewives and mothers' (St Croix, 2009: 304) and they required adherence to a strict set of rules.

There were also a number of more radical organisations such as the Woodcraft Folk (founded in 1925) that were set up with pacifist and socialist values, which, although they shared 'the environmental values and many of the methods of Scouting [they] opposed its imperialist origins' (St Croix, 2009: 304). More radical youth work was often developed by politically marginalised people, such as the pacifists during the Second World War, who were working with economically and socially disadvantaged young people and saw them as 'creators not consumers' (Smith, 1988: 46) of a more socially just society. Other organisations that were concerned with developing young people's political understanding of power relations in society included the early Cooperative Youth Movement, the Young Socialists and the Socialist Sunday Schools. This latter movement began in the 1890s in Scotland and the aim was to teach socialist values to children so that 'socialist beliefs continued from one generation to another' (Fisher, 1999: 136). Later social movements such as the Women's and Black Consciousness Movements developed in the 1970s. In all these cases more radical educational opportunities were seen as a way of helping young people to:

> understand their experiences of oppression as being both personal and political [so] they can, as a consequence, take action in both the way they live their lives and in the political arena. (Smith, 1988: 56)

There were, and are, many traditions in youth work and these are but a small example designed to show how these early movements have impacted on community education today. It is also important to remember that, whatever the concerns of the organisers of provision, young people have the ability to disrupt their best efforts and take what they want out of it. This means that, as Mark Smith points out, 'youth work cannot be portrayed as exhibiting a simple one-way imposition of middle-class values and behaviours upon the working-class young' (Smith, 1988: 20). It is in the interactions between the purposes of providers and those of the recipients that practice develops.

Involving adults

Just like youth work, the early development of education for adults came from competing traditions that had different ideological purposes. One tradition was derived from the radical working-class movements in the first half of the nineteenth century who used education to provide an understanding of their existing circumstances so that they could change them. Radical men and women of the time argued that 'knowledge lies everywhere to hand for those who observe and think' (Holyoake, 1896: 4) and saw education as about 'the struggles of everyday life ... and as a cooperative effort based on fellowship' (Burke, 2009: 67). They argued that in order to preserve their independence 'we must do it for ourselves' and win what they regarded as real knowledge rather than the knowledge passed down from above (Johnson, 1988: 79).

In many ways the 'radicals' were reacting to what Ian Bryant describes as the 'respectable' tradition where education for the 'moral improvement' of the servant classes was advocated and supported by members of the affluent classes (Bryant, 1984: 5–7). One of the cultural roots of this tradition can be traced back to the influence of Calvinism and Presbyterianism where the ideals of thrift, discipline and self-improvement generated a culture that supported education as a means of acquiring spiritual salvation and material advancement (Crowther and Martin, 2006: 20). Another root of the respectable tradition was the demand for both a more skilled and also a more docile labour force as a result of the rapid industrialisation of manufacturing in the nineteenth century. This required people to be better educated and so some of the more enlightened employers took it upon themselves to educate their employees and their families who would in turn become employees. The pioneer for this work was Robert Owen in the New Lanark Mills who opened an 'Institute for the Formation of

Character' in 1816. In his opening address Owen said that it was designed to change a number of existing practices including:

> drunkenness, injustice in your transactions, want of charity for the opinions of others, and mistaken notions, in which you had been instructed, as to the superiority of your religious opinions, and that these were calculated to produce more happiness than any of the opinions impressed on the minds of an infinitely more numerous part of mankind. (Owen, 1816)

The Institute was therefore based on benevolent paternalism aimed at fitting the village youth for the world of work in the mills, saving the adults from the more radical forms of education offered by secular organisations and thus posing no threat to the existing order of society (Donnachie, 2003). Owen used a variety of methods to develop good character, including providing a basic education for the young children of New Lanark, evening classes for the adults and older children with dancing, music and military exercise 'as one means of reforming vicious habits ... by promoting cheerfulness and contentment, and thus diverting attention from things that are vile and degrading' (Owen, quoted in Donnachie, 2003). His vision was that education would make good citizens of men and women through providing an environment in which their better natures would be encouraged to grow, with the body and mind both well cared for and trained in productive habits and ways of living (Cole, 1930). Again there are echoes of the concern that the providers of opportunities for young people had for ensuring that physical, cultural and intellectual stimulus was provided to help develop more bourgeois values.

The 1850s and 1860s were a period of relative prosperity and employers across the UK attempted to woo skilled workers by sponsoring libraries, educational lectures on science, history and culture, and social and musical activities. These activities were often linked with the Temperance movement as many employers shared Owen's concerns about his employees' drunkenness (Cooke, 2006) and so, by the 1860s, Temperance societies had been established by many of the large-scale manufacturers. One historian suggested that the Temperance movement had the 'short term aim of increasing the usefulness of skilled workers ... and the long term aim of spreading bourgeois values' (Pollard, 1963: 268) but Anthony Cooke argues that 'for many workers it was a grassroots movement, linked to economic survival and self respect' (2006: 115). The outcomes of this and other social movements of the period were influenced by how much democratic control the workers had over the organisation.

The early part of the twentieth century saw the growth of both 'respectable' and 'radical' education under the influence of the labour and cooperative movement. For example, in the 'respectable' tradition the Glasgow Cooperative Society had, by 1910, a thriving lending library, reading rooms, choirs and a women's guild that provided classes in dressmaking, fancy work and other 'domestic virtues' (Cooke, 2006: 129). However, many adults who were unskilled or were not involved in large-scale manufacturing remained untouched by any form of organised educational effort because the main providers 'overestimated ordinary people's educational background but underestimated their intelligence' by delivering lectures that patronised their audience (Bryant, 1984: 9).

During this period socialist educators, such as John MacLean, led 'radical' education and this group gave evening classes in the Glasgow engineering shops and the Clydeside shipyards to workers' study groups. The curriculum was framed by Marxist texts and the aim was to equip workers' leaders intellectually to play their part in the anticipated revolution (Crowther and Martin, 2006: 20). MacLean contrasted this form of learning with education designed to 'increase efficiency … to make better wage slaves or better producers of commodities', whereas his aim was to 'see that all public educational institutions are used for the creation of intelligent, class-conscious workers' (quoted in Bryant, 1984: 10). The rival organisation, the Workers' Educational Association (WEA), established in Scotland in 1908, was regarded with distain by the socialists because it adopted a more personal enrichment ideology. However, it was also concerned with helping workers gain an awareness of social and political affairs and was geared towards providing an education for working people to become social and political leaders (Bryant, 1984:10).

In contrast, the respectable tradition in Scotland in the first half of the twentieth century was linked with the slow growth of university extra-mural provision—a patchwork of liberal adult education, leisure and interest-based courses provided mainly by the ancient Scottish universities—and local authority adult classes. The other important strand of adult provision (or, more accurately, training) was 'night classes' which offered certificated vocational courses, mainly in further education colleges. In statistical terms, more people were probably involved in this kind of vocational training than all other forms of adult education put together (Bryant, 1984: 14).

It is important, however, not to make a simple distinction between these traditions, because in reality the overlap between them has been reformulated and reconfigured over time. This is partly due to changing currents of social and political struggle where both traditions have had some influence on the provision made by local authorities and further and higher education in catering for marginalised communities. For example, the growth of new social movements from the 1970's, especially the peace, women's and environmental movements, 'reinvigorated organisations like the WEA and refocused their social purpose' much more on social change (Crowther and Martin, 2006: 20).

Working with poor communities

Work in poor communities has its roots in the early social reforms in health, housing, social work, local government and town planning carried out in the late nineteenth century in response to the growing discontent of the new urban poor (Yeo and Yeo, 1988). In a similar way to work with young people, early provision was carried out through philanthropic efforts with the most prominent body, the Charity Organisation Society (COS), being established in 1869 (Leat, 1975). A particular concern was the lack of self-reliance amongst the poor and the suggested solution was to strengthen character and encourage independence by working to change *individuals* rather than the circumstances they were experiencing. One of the founders of COS, Canon Samuel Barnett, went on to establish the University Settlement Movement that was designed to be:

> the means by which men or women may share themselves with their neighbours; a club-house in an industrial district, where the condition of membership is the performance of a citizen's duty; a house among the poor, where residents may make friends with the poor. (Barnett, 1898: 26)

Barnett's vision was that these natural leaders would help to bring about social order in the densely populated urban areas in ways that would avoid the potential for dissidence. However, he did have a more structural view of the reason why people were not practising self-help than the members of COS because he viewed people's social problems as a *consequence* of poverty rather than as caused by character defects (Shaw, 2003). Settlements aimed to convert 'the crowded, squalid and featureless inner city into active and coherent neighbourhoods' (Rose, 2001: 27) through the creation of a village within an urban slum as a return to the rural idyll. People from the more articulate and prosperous classes were expected to act as role models of civic leadership and 'improve the character of the poor by example' (Craig *et al.*, 1982: 1). Three key areas for action were identified by the Settlements: for scientific research concerning poverty; the furthering of wider lives through education; and an enhancement of leadership in local communities (Pimlott, 1935: 11). The first Settlement, Toynbee Hall, attracted a number of very able and committed settlers, many of whom became deeply involved with developing policy around the alleviation of poverty as a result of their research into its causes and included William Beveridge and R. H. Tawney who were instrumental in establishing the British Welfare State (Smith, 2007).

Community work in the UK is also embedded in the history of British imperialism and colonialism where the growing independence movements led to the recognition, after the Second World War, that there was a need for social and economic development to meet the new political and social expectations of the working classes (Shaw, 2003: 13). Community development techniques were used primarily as a method of both ensuring the growth of democratic institutions based on the British model and integrating colonial territories into the capitalist economic order. Mayo (1975) argued that this form of community development fulfilled political, economic and ideological functions for the British state through the incorporation of local populations into the development project. It was assumed that the promotion of economic competition would encourage self-reliance, self-regulation and self-surveillance and this was achieved by manipulating local cultural patterns of mutuality. However, colonialism did not always go unchallenged and the community development process led in some cases to the promotion of popular education and to the establishment of solidarity resulting in anti-colonial struggles. For example, the work of Julius Nyerere in Tanganyika who brought together a number of different nationalist factions into one grouping that eventually led to the creation of the Republic of Tanzania in 1964 (Samoff, 1990).

So, just like work with young people, attempts at incorporating people into particular practices led to resistance as well as compliance. As David Jones argued:

> While from one side community work is concerned with the encouragement of local initiative and local decision making, from the other it is a means of implementing and expediting national policies at the local level. (Jones, 1981: 7)

This ambiguity at the heart of community work lies both between the intentions and the outcomes of policy and also within the dynamic relationship between individuals' capacity to make change and the restrictions on that capacity. This means that it is open to a variety of ideological interpretations that can range from 'conservative strategies for social control … to more overtly revolutionary strategies' (Craig *et al.*, 1982:1).

Community

As can be seen from this brief review of the antecedents of community education the reaction to the social fragmentation brought about by the industrialisation and urbanisation in the nineteenth century led to a wide variety of provision for young people, adults and communities. The ideology behind this provision created tensions between the solutions offered in response to major social and economic changes from dominant groups who were concerned to prevent dissidence and the different ideas of those that were excluded from power who were more interested in changing the status quo. These tensions were played out in all these different contexts where community-based interventions were practised. In this section these tensions will be further interrogated through an exploration of how the concept of 'community' is understood.

Although the word has been in the English language since the fourteenth century, the concept was first explored in the nineteenth century by German social theorists, especially Ferdinand Tonnies who developed the concepts of *Gemeinschaft* and *Gesellschaft* to describe two different forms of human relationships (Tonnies, [1887] 1957). Both are difficult to translate exactly, but *Gemeinschaft* relationships were characteristically based on a common locale, kinship and friendships that were intimate, taken for granted and where values were shared and unchallenged by outside influences and pressures. On the other hand *Gesellschaft* relationships were more distant and impersonal and derived from the public world of work where relationships were generally voluntary and were related to a particular role or task. *Gesellschaft* relationships were particularly affected by geographical and social mobility because they required increasingly specialised roles and tasks.

The ideal of the *Gemeinschaft* type community was based on nostalgia for the familiar world that had been disrupted by the fragmentation brought about by the increasingly complex society developing at the time. It was a retreat to earlier times where values and beliefs were prescribed and people were protected from disturbing outside ideas and influences and did not have to grapple with situations to which there were no ready answers. This concept has, however, gone on informing thinking about the nature of community especially the association of the term with 'warm' and desirable values and a view of 'us' against 'them'. Yet, as Mae Shaw (2008: 25) points out, this conservative view was only one tradition and it coexisted at the time with an alternative revolutionary socialist ideology expressed through the French communes and the development of communism. So these competing visions of what community means have created separate discourses that vie for legitimacy in policy and practice leading to Raymond Williams' suggestion that the problem of 'community' was that it 'can be the warmly persuasive word to describe an existing set of relationships, or the warmly persuasive word to describe an alternative set of relationships' (1976: 66).

It seems that if *the* definition of community is looked for then the critical connection between how community is valued and what function it fulfils in particular contexts is missed. This is why it is important to consider 'its actual use in language and thought, in the description, interpretation, organisation and evaluation of behaviour' (Plant, 1974: 10). So the ways in which 'community' is used as a descriptive category are first considered and then how the concept is interpreted in policy is explored.

Community as a descriptive category can be broadly divided into three main areas of meaning:

- Place or locality—this is the most frequently used meaning and refers to people who have in common that they live in a particular geographical community such as a neighbourhood or village.
- Interest—this refers to people who are linked together by factors such as religious belief, sexual orientation or ethnic origin and so they share a common characteristic such as their membership of the Christian, Gay or Chinese communities.
- Function—this refers to groups with the same profession, such as teachers, or the same role, such as community representatives, or those who have common interests such as football, which leads them to acquire a common sense of identity through the actions that they engage in together.

From these uses of the term it can be seen that 'community' involves boundaries, because if the members of a group have something in common with each other that is going to distinguish them in a significant way from the members of other possible groups. The boundaries may be physical, religious or linguistic and, as Cohen argues, 'they may [also] be thought of as existing in the minds of the beholders' (Cohen, 1985: 12). Community thus implies both similarity and difference and so it is an idea that focuses on relationships. However, it is important to think about how boundaries also construct difference where particular groups such as asylum seekers or disabled people can be seen as 'the other'—'to be tolerated as conditional members only' (Shaw, 2008: 29). This suggests that, far from generating positive social relations, community can reinforce 'social polarisation and potential conflict' (Shaw, 2008: 29) as happens in, for example, 'the Mafia'.

There has been a continuing tendency to romanticise the neighbourhood concept of community based on the assumption that the relationships between people and the social networks of which they are a part are characterised by close bonds and mutuality between neighbours. This romantic notion also assumes that people have choice in where they live. However, many people live in places that Mae Shaw (2008) describes as 'contrived' communities that have been created out of economic, rather than social, needs. This happens when social policies operate to confine people to particular geographical areas such as large peripheral housing estates leading to segregation that is based on class, gender or race. In this case, as she goes on to argue, it is clear that 'place structures social relations, just as, conversely, social (and economic) relations structure the parameters of choice in relation to place' (Shaw, 2008: 31). For example, women who are bringing their children up by themselves may have no choice in where they live because the only housing available to them is social housing in economically poor areas that are often far from their friends and relatives. A further critique of the concept of 'neighbourhood as community' (Harvey, 1989; Williams, 1993) is that if community is constructed mainly as a place then this obscures the ways in which the spatial segregation that is caused by redevelopment may cause people to accept their 'place' as subordinate.

Another way of thinking about community is to see it as playing a symbolic role in generating people's sense of belonging. Habermas (1989) has argued that as society is increasingly administered at a level remote from the input of its citizens, individuals draw from custom and cultural traditions to construct their identities, define situations and create social solidarity. The boundaries between the personal 'life world' of the individual and the 'systems world' of the state and its interventions mean that 'community' represents a form of social organisation that is situated, and mediates, between these two worlds of the public and private and of the individual and society. Others have suggested that the sense of belonging derived from community may express itself more as a desire and aspiration than as a reality. Jeremy Brent, for example, argues that 'community is the continually reproduced desire to overcome the adversity of social life' (Brent, 2004: 221) and he sees community as not fixed or static but rather based on people's responses to changing circumstances. So people may construct community for themselves in response to common needs and problems where they can express their freedom in and through the associations they form. In these cases communities are constructed by the common experience of exclusion from a wide range of social, economic, political and cultural resources and activities that many other people may take for granted.

The conceptual confusion surrounding 'community' coupled with its positive connotations means that it can be used politically to encourage acceptance of policy initiatives by creating, in Ian Martin's words, 'a smokescreen to fudge some of the key issues ... about power, accountability and resource allocation' (1987: 13). So, rather than people choosing their own communities they may have a particular community thrust upon them by policy-makers who are interested in managing and regulating people. On the other hand, communities can also be constructed by groups of people coming together around common issues and identities through pursuing their own interests that become concrete as the result of joint action. As new projects are undertaken the boundaries around the action move and so these constructed communities become dynamic spaces in which people's lived experiences can be worked out.

So, clearly, the word 'community' is a difficult notion to understand but remains an idea that is important because it describes something essential and irreducible about the everyday reality of people's lives and the spaces where those lives are lived. It also means that those that are engaged in the practice of community education need to be clear about how they are defining community and the relationships within communities because these definitions have strong implications for action. At one extreme they might choose an essentially hierarchical, socially regressive and static model of human relations based on a conservative, nostalgic view of community or at the other extreme a model that is progressive, emancipatory and dynamic.

Conclusion

This chapter has discussed the antecedents of community education as work that takes place outside of formal institutions and responds to the notion of community. It has shown how it has developed out of a range of ideologies broadly concerned with maintaining or challenging the status quo. One strand has focused on philanthropic concerns for the welfare of disadvantaged people partly in response to fears of loss of social control by the more powerful groups in society and partly out of concerns for the economic and social development of the workforce. On the other hand, radical groups such as the socialist, peace or the women's movements have sought to challenge existing notions by gaining control over education in order to change the world for the better.

Another aspect of the chapter has been an exploration of the variety of ways in which different understandings of 'community' have shaped both practice and policy. The different assumptions about the purpose, role and focus of the antecedents of community education over time have been examined and it appears that in practice, much provision is a dynamic hybrid with a capacity for accommodating and fusing different and contradictory ideas and values. This means that the purposes behind education within and for communities should always be treated as being subject to interrogation and revision 'as a process of social and political negotiation' (Shaw, 2003: 1).

As Ian Martin (1999) has argued, the practices that come under the umbrella of community education operate at the 'meso' level between the individual and the state, the local and the global, the personal and the wider society. Community education, through a focus on responding to people's own concerns, works to create a shared, active and political space where wider solidarities that encompass a multiplicity of perspectives can be developed. In this space interactive communication can explore and challenge the boundaries of difference, whilst searching out a common cause. This conceptualisation shifts the focus from working with people in similar situations and locations in homogenous communities—Tonnies' *Gemeinschaft* relationships—to working with people in different situations and spaces but with similar issues. This involves acting collaboratively to develop a common understanding and a sense of a shared fate out of which solidarity can be forged. This common fate can be at the global level through, for example, an understanding of the impact of climate change on all peoples but it is also worked out in the micro-practices of everyday life through lived experiences.

It is important to understand how the meaning of 'community' in policy discourses changes over time because of the implications for educational interventions. This is because, at its most basic, community is essentially shared, lived experience. Changes in community education that reflect new contexts, contingencies and competing interests come about through what is emphasised, and what is omitted, in policy and practice. In turn these presences and absences work to shape particular social ends. For example, community education can serve to co-opt potential troublemakers by absorbing the energy of local activists in residents' associations that have been imposed externally rather than identifying common interests and issues that communities have chosen as important for themselves. On the other hand, if the community educator nurtures a joint purpose formed around issues derived from common experiences of exclusion, then communities can become active creations focusing on joint action. In this case action is required that encourages people to express their communality rather than simply their self-interest so that they can come together in solidarity. From this perspective, as Michael Apple argues, community education becomes an 'act of repositioning [that] in essence says that the best way to understand what any set of institutions, policies and practices does, is to see it from the standpoint of those who have the least power' (Apple, 2006: 229).

In an attempt to do this the next chapter will explore in detail how community education has developed in Scotland through an examination of the assumptions behind government policies and the ensuing practice developments. The focus will be on the spaces that these policies create for making a real difference to the lives of people.

Chapter 2

Community Education in Scotland

> For many years Scotland has been admired and envied for its achievements in education ... But somewhere along the line education has ceased to capture the imagination of a large part of the Scottish population ... we want to make a reality of educational opportunity for all. (Donald Dewar, *Opportunity Scotland*, Scottish Executive, 1998a: 1)

Introduction

Community education has developed out of varied educational experiences that served many different, and at times conflicting, purposes, so that it has been difficult to arrive at and agree a definition that draws on this heritage. The previous chapter showed that different ideologies underpinned earlier work with young people and adults in communities and this chapter argues that these reformist and radical traditions are still present in the work today. What is included in policy as well as what is excluded, however, shapes practice through emphasising the particular issues that need to be dealt with. In order to examine how the policy agenda has shaped practice a short history of developments in Scotland since community education was first established in 1975 is provided.

In the beginning

The Alexander Report *Adult Education: The Challenge of Change* (SED, 1975), that led to the setting up of the Community Education Service in Scottish Regional and Island Authorities, was originally established by the Scottish Education Department to examine the role of non-vocational adult education. The recommendations of the Alexander Report were strongly influenced by an understanding that adult education should help to counter the disadvantage experienced by a range of groups including older people, lone parents, unemployed people,

early school leavers and minority ethnic communities. Participation in community education was expected to enable these groups and individuals to 'develop
their capacities for a full and rich personal life' as well as helping them to adapt to
the 'pace at which new knowledge and attitudes are diffused' (SED, 1975: 26). It
was suggested that educational intervention should aim to minimise the impedi-
ments to participation experienced by many adults and that there 'should be a
transfer of emphasis from teaching to learning' (SED, 1975: 24). Adult education provision was in a relatively weak position in Scotland at this time, but youth
and community work had been significantly expanded from the late 1960s and
was a well-established part of local authorities' provision. This led the committee
to suggest that the mechanism for expanding adult education should be to use
the locally responsive provision, underpinned by a commitment to inter-agency
strategies, provided by the Youth and Community Service. These two services,
however, had very different ideological roots and cultural practices, with adult
education tending to provide formal classes in specific subjects and youth and
community work tending to place more emphasis on informal, leisure-based
activities. Colin Kirkwood caricatured them in this way:

> Adult education was organised by men in suits ... who ran classes in
> evening institutes, usually in schools and at night ... They saw them-
> selves as educators. The youth service was different. It was also run by
> males but they tended to be more informal, with open necked shirts.
> They ran youth clubs with table tennis, dancing, football and other
> sports. (Kirkwood, 1990: 295)

However, despite these differences, the Alexander Committee saw a number
of pragmatic reasons why the two services should be brought together. One
reason was that youth and community workers were seen as being closer to the
people than the traditional subject-centred and institution-based adult education service. Another was that the joining of adult education together with a
numerically far stronger youth and community service, rich in buildings and
staff, was expected to provide a range of contacts and understanding to which
adult educators could respond. Thus the Report sought to create the conditions though which adult education could move from being the leisure pursuit
of an affluent minority to becoming a more relevant and locally based enter-
prise that involved the mass of people who had traditionally not participated
in its provision.

The key recommendation of the Report was that 'adult education should be regarded as an aspect of community education and should, with the youth and community service, be incorporated into a community education service' (SED, 1975: 35). The 'challenge of change' that it posed to this new service was to escape from the conventional syllabi of school-based evening classes that had involved less than 4% of the population, largely from its older, better educated and more affluent members. Instead the new service, which was to be highly professional, was to create a more relevant curriculum within communities that, by their very power of appeal and relevance, would stimulate participation in education. The Report consistently argued for change and qualitative improvement and redirection rather than an expansion that was more of the same.

The publication of the Alexander Report was timed to coincide with local government reform and the advent of the new large local authorities in Scotland. These large-scale units would, it was assumed, provide an adequate resource base for the development and expansion of the new service. The Alexander recommendations reflected the common approach of the time that looked for economies of scale and strategic planning. At the same time it counter-balanced centralisation with a 'concern to foster local democracy by encouraging devolution, accountability and participation at the local level' (Martin, 1996: 132). The locally based Community Education Service would, in the Alexander Committee's view, have an important part to play in nurturing a pluralist democracy by helping to manage the tension between the policies of the state and the politics of communities. These were often in conflict as the state sought to reduce public expenditure and communities sought to retain their rights. The central concern of the Report was to address issues of social and educational disadvantage. This meant that the challenge for adult education was to increase its capacity to respond to the interests and needs of the groups that were most likely to suffer the negative consequences of economic change and, potentially, to become more alienated and disaffected from the political process.

The outcome of the Report was the establishment of an integrated Community Education Service in most of the new Scottish Regional and Island authorities. The work of such services was to be characterised by local community-oriented approaches with a pronounced emphasis on positive discrimination in favour of traditionally non-participant groups. Sir Kenneth Alexander, reflecting back on his committee's recommendations, confirmed that the basic intention was that adult education's use of the youth work base in communities 'should create a wider

network within which more people could become aware of educational opportunities' (1993: 36). The Report conceived of adult educators and youth workers
as 'committed allies' with a 'common purpose' and recommended substantial
investment in new appointments, training and research in adult education. These
new appointments would equalise the relationship with youth workers, who out-
numbered adult educators by a ratio of seven to one (Kirkwood, 1990: 297). This
requirement was never met. As a consequence, rather than identifying a 'common
core of knowledge and expertise', work was carried out in three central areas—
informal educational work with young people, community based adult education
and community development work. Few of the people undertaking this work had
had any further professional training and so continued to work within their existing traditions. It was soon realised that if changes were to occur in practice then
new forms of pre-service and in-service training had to be available.

The emergence of genericism

The Alexander committee had expected that training would enable an increase in
specialisation. However, the first report to address the issue of training, chaired by
Lady Carnegie (SED, 1977), instead advocated an increase in generic training. This
was a clear departure from the proposals made by the committee and diminished
the existing strengths of the adult educators and youth and community workers
by emphasising the common core of knowledge and skills required for community
education. The Carnegie Report also made grand claims about community education through presenting an idealising description of what it could do:

> The significance of community education for the well being of society,
> for the quality of life in communities, and for the personal fulfilment
> of individuals is now widely recognized. (SED, 1977: 7)

Such claims were clearly inflated. The service had only just started and there
was no evidence of its efficacy. They were probably trying to 'hype community
education in order to gain extra resources in a time of economic stringency'
(Kirkwood, 1990: 302). However, these grand claims meant there was the
danger of a gap opening up between claim and performance so that community
education might be setting itself up to fail.

The next report about training was developed by the Scottish Community
Education Council and was called *Training for Change* (SCEC, 1984).
'Community education' was described as an umbrella term that had at its heart

a process that involved 'purposive developmental and educational programmes and structures which afford opportunities for individual and collective growth and change throughout life' (SCEC, 1984: 3). The Report acknowledged that workers would need more in-depth knowledge of particular areas of community education and one proposal was that there should be more training time spent in fieldwork practice. Generally the pattern of training proposed was to enable the community educator to fulfil a variety of roles. These included working 'as an educator, as a communicator, as a facilitator, as a manager and as a trainer of part-time and voluntary colleagues' (McConnell, 1996: 213). As well as these varied roles the Report also sketched out the range of additional responsibilities that community education had gained in the eight years since the publication of the Alexander Report. It was now covering adult basic education, vocational train-ing, women's education, children's play, older people and community schools, as well as the original functions. *Training for Change*, in the light of all these new responsibilities, summarised community education as a 'rapidly expanding field of practice'. Surprisingly, however, the committee did not complain that few extra resources had been supplied to fulfil these increased responsibilities. It merely tried to come up with a training programme that would encompass all these areas. In order to do this the Report recommended a 'core and options model of training, in which generic training formed the core and the training in specific settings [and the broad arenas of adult education, community work and youth work] formed the options' (McConnell, 1996: 215).

Colin Kirkwood assesses the Report as reflecting the 'anxiety of the profession about the core of its identity … and the absence of boundaries around its core business' (Kirkwood, 1990: 306). Welding together professions with very differ-ent traditions into something that has clear common objectives takes time and resources that were certainly not available to this developing service. It is thus hardly surprising that a detailed study of practice in the Community Education Service carried out in the early 1980s by David Alexander and colleagues (Alexander *et al.*, 1984) suggested that the development of generic approaches had negative effects on the adult education elements of the work. In their view this was mainly because the dominance of youth work traditions of non-direc-tion and facilitative group work impeded systematic learning by the participants in the provision. According to Ian Martin (1996: 135), this meant that 'the edu-cational elements of the service's work tended to be presented in covert, or at least very oblique, terms with learning seen as an incidental accretion'.

Expectations and resources

During the 1980s the local authorities, particularly the large Regions of Strathclyde, Lothian and Tayside, put more resources into community education because it was seen as taking the lead in regenerating disadvantaged geographical communities that had high levels of poverty and unemployment. This led to the creation of 'a community development arm of education departments that encouraged the identification of local need, the design of appropriate programmes and services and the engagement of local people in their delivery' (Milburn, 1999: 838). The local authorities also invested more in training and professional development for their employees and this is turn resulted in more educationally focused pre-qualifying training courses (COSLA, 1995). All these changes in professional development gave a stronger emphasis to the role of learning and education, rather than leisure activities, with the process of community engagement seen as about promoting change in communities and individuals. Priorities switched from leisure and subject-based provision to more community-based and issue-orientated activities with the focus on how people could identify and take action about local issues. Community educators became more skilled at involving people in learning through building on what people already knew and could do. Previously unsupported groups who were hard to reach, such as young people contacted through street work, became included in learning opportunities (Hendry et al., 1991: 79). There was also a switch from more formal educational provision that took place in classes to much more informal learning that could take place through discussions and conversations with, for example, young people on street corners (Hendry et al., 1991: 79). The communities into which community educators intervened were usually designated as 'disadvantaged' because of their socio-economic position, but the focus was on how the richness of the ideas, cooperative values and practical self-help available in the community could be mobilised (Milburn, 1999).

There was a considerable growth in the numbers of community educators, so that by the mid-1990s there were over 1,500 employed by local authorities (in education departments and to a lesser extent in social work, neighbourhood, community and leisure services) and in the non-governmental voluntary sector. These professionals supported tens of thousands of part-time and voluntary staff and their overall aim was to engage with people within geographical communities and communities of interest in order to:

identify needs, to motivate individuals and groups to acquire new knowledge, skills and confidence, and to promote learning that was enjoyable, relevant, accessible and empowering to the participating learners. (McConnell, 1996: 3)

Less than 3% of total educational expenditure in Scottish local authorities went on community education at this time. The typical community educator worked within a community of several thousand people. One reason that community education attracted such a small proportion of the education budget was the lack of a legislative base that made it a requirement that community education was provided. This weak position meant that when local government was reorganised in 1995 into small unitary authorities the provision of community education across Scotland was reduced. Few could afford the sophisticated central services of the now defunct Regional Authorities. Many local authorities were forced to cut staff, close community buildings, reduce programmes and even shut down altogether some aspects of their provision such as community-based adult education. In a number of authorities the community education service and other council services were amalgamated to form new departments such as Community and Leisure Services, Neighbourhood Services, Community Services or Community Economic and Development Services. These amalgamations resulted in new department heads with different outlooks. Some did not see the work of community educators as inherently educational even though it might make a considerable difference to communities (see Milburn, 1999: 844).

The impact of the reorganisation of local government on the Community Education Service generated concern within the Scottish local and central governmental bodies because they recognised that the provision of community education opportunities had declined in some areas by nearly 50%. There was a direct correlation between this reduction in staffing and the reduction in participation by the most socially excluded groups. For example, adult basic education participants declined by 40% between 1992 and 1996/7. This realisation led to a report from the Convention of Scottish Local Authorities (COSLA) that called for community educators to adopt a more issues-focused and developmental role (COSLA, 1998). The Report argued, in ways that echoed the Alexander Report of 20 years earlier, that 'the service had been influenced by providing for those who, in part, could pay; a market rather than a needs-led response' (COSLA, 1998: 7). The role suggested for community education was essentially about enhancing the confidence and capacity of individuals, community groups and other professional colleagues both within and outwith the local authority sector. The emphasis was to be on 'people-centred development' (COSLA, 1998: 11) especially for those that were most disadvantaged. The Report made a number of recommendations, including a strengthened statutory duty to provide community education and for the revision of funding arrangements, but neither of these was implemented. The track record of Scottish governments in failing to take on board anything that increased costs thus continued unbroken.

Orphan to mainstream?

These concerns about the future of community education led to the setting up of another working group by the Scottish Office chaired by HM Senior Chief Inspector of Schools Douglas Osler. Its remit was 'to consider a national strategy for community based adult education, youth work and educational support for community development' (Scottish Office, 1998a: 5). The vision developed by Osler for what community education should achieve in Scotland was 'that all of its citizens, in particular those who are socially excluded, [should be able] to develop their potential to the full and to have the capacity, individually and collectively, to meet the challenge of change' (Scottish Office, 1998a: 14). The similarity to the language of the Alexander Report was not accidental. The concerns about the changing demands on the workforce caused by technological innovations and the growing inequality between the poor and the wealthy that had influenced Alexander's committee also impacted on Osler. However, whilst Alexander had emphasised that 'the right of opposition to and criticism of the government of the day and other forms of authority is fundamental to a pluralist society' (SED, 1975: 26) Osler simply referred to Scotland as a 'democratic and socially just society' (Scottish Office, 1998a: 14). However, this rhetorical statement contradicted the evidence of growing inequalities that were concentrated in particular geographic areas characterised by high unemployment (HM Treasury, 1999).

When community education was a new profession its advocates often over-claimed the changes it could bring about, but this tendency was now echoed by government Ministers. So in launching this Report (in November 1998) Helen Liddell, Minister of State at the Scottish Office, said:

> All ages and all social groups in communities across Scotland will
> benefit from the Government's approach that is to move community

education from the status of 'orphan' to mainstream provision. Education is this Government's number one priority and community education is at the very heart of this. (Scottish Office, 1998b: 1–2)

This transformation was to take place, however, through changing a few structures such as 'developing community-learning plans that assessed the range of professional expertise available and the procedures for ensuring that staff from different service areas worked together in communities' (SOEID, 1999: 5.23). The focus was to be on addressing the learning needs associated with social inclusion, lifelong learning and citizenship. This seemed to suggest that moving to the mainstream was really about integrating the work of community education much more closely with the agenda of the Scottish Executive and limiting its activities to their priorities.

Another aspect of the Report was that the local authorities were exhorted to improve the skills of its community education staff (SOEID, 1999: 5.23). The assumption was that the huge task of 'addressing the needs of alienated young people' or 'promoting healthier life styles' or 'developing core skills' (SOEID, 1999: 4.44) was to be solved by improving the skills of individual community educators rather than tackling the socio-economic structures that caused the problems in the first place.

This emphasis on the profession's lack of skills led to the establishment of a group to review training for community education and its Report was called *Empowered to Practice* (Scottish Executive, 2000a). The group advocated the use of the term 'community learning and development' as this would 'bring together the best of what has been done under the banners of "community education" and "community development"'. The main aim of community learning and development was, it was argued, 'to help individuals and communities tackle real issues in their lives through community action and community-based learning' (Scottish Executive, 2002: 11). The Scottish Executive expressed concerns that those providing key services for people in 'deprived communities were not sufficiently skilled or focused on community regeneration' (Scottish Executive, 2002: 11). Thus the work of community educators was firmly tied back into communities of place and strongly linked to the regeneration of 'deprived' communities.

The Scottish Executive enthusiastically adopted the term 'community learning and development' and in 2004 they issued a circular called *Working and Learning Together to Build Stronger Communities*, generally known as WALT

(Communities Scotland and Scottish Executive, 2004), that defined the new national priorities using this term. The priorities were: achievement through learning for adults and young people and achievement through building community capacity. In WALT, Community learning and development (CLD) was characterised as 'an approach', a common defining feature of which was 'that programmes and activities are [to be] developed in dialogue with communities and participants' (Communities Scotland and Scottish Executive, 2004: 7). CLD was also seen 'as a key tool in delivering ... social justice [through] supporting strategies aimed at closing the opportunity gap ... and encouraging community regeneration' (Communities Scotland and Scottish Executive, 2004: 2). In comparing the guidance that informed the operation of community education given in 1999 and that provided in 2004, it is clear that there was much more focus on targeting provision and interventions at the most 'disadvantaged individuals and groups' (Communities Scotland and Scottish Executive, 2004: 3) and at communities of place rather than communities of interest or function leading to a narrowing of the scope of the work.

There was also great significance in the change of language from community *education* to community *learning and development*. The emphasis on learning was partly due to the newer theories of learning that showed the importance of 'the active role of students in the construction of knowledge and understanding and [consequently] the more facilitating role of teachers in this' (Biesta, 2009: 38). However, this change in language also reflected a shift to the more individualistic concept of 'learning' in contrast to 'education', because the latter term always implies a relationship between the educator and the student. Moreover, the role of educator is to provide guiding ideas about the purpose, content and direction of the learning that is expected to take place. The curriculum that is developed can then be negotiated with the participants, but if these underpinning ideas are hidden then it is less open. If the emphasis is only on learning as a process there is a lack of recognition that it matters what people learn and what they learn it for. It also means ignoring the fact that 'education can be difficult and challenging, rather than a smooth process that aims to meet the supposed "needs" of the learner' (Biesta, 2009: 39).

A focus on outcomes

Another way in which the scope of community education was being narrowed was through a focus on outcomes. Just like other forms of education, its practice was being affected during the early 2000s by the dominant view of central government that the best way of judging the effectiveness of provision was to pay attention to outputs and performance. As Janet Newman and colleagues have pointed out, this view has led to more emphasis on the 'regulation of standards and systems for guiding decision-making and assessment ... [and] imply an instrumental view of policy ... that assumes people and organisations act rationally within narrow conceptions of self-interest' (Newman *et al.*, 2008: 538). They further argue that this model puts an emphasis on compliance rather than commitment and so is ineffective when policy problems are complex and require a strong value base and organisational culture. Community education/CLD clearly comes under this latter category but the profession was under pressure at the time to be 'able to assess more clearly the contribution of CLD to achieving outcomes' (Communities Scotland and Scottish Executive, 2004: 23) and demonstrate the difference that its interventions had made. There was a concern, by government, that there was insufficient knowledge of the changes that had resulted from community education activities and that this needed to be addressed through accountability systems based on externally verifiable data. A framework was therefore developed entitled *Delivering Change: Understanding the Outcomes of Community Learning and Development* (Communities Scotland and Scottish Executive 2007). The document acknowledged that the work of CLD was both long term and difficult to measure since its overall purpose was 'to improve the quality of life for individuals and communities' and pointed out that it was 'not reasonable for people working in CLD to be totally responsible for end outcomes' such as 'improving employability' (Communities Scotland and Scottish Executive, 2007: 8). This was a new departure, since it appeared that up to this point grand claims about the contribution of community education/CLD had been made and expected. At the same time, however, outcomes and targets were tightly specified and so their achievement or otherwise was much more open to scrutiny and regulation.

The document provided a framework for assessing the intermediate outcomes of CLD under the headings of personal development and community capacity building. It was acknowledged that 'CLD is built on the principle that learners and communities are at the heart of this work [and] it is their aims that the work focuses on' (Communities Scotland and Scottish Executive, 2007: 3) and so the range of outcomes were meant to help practitioners choose appropriately for their work and situation. However, the assessment of outcomes was also tied into the HM Inspectorate of Education indicators of quality in their inspection framework and so the outcomes were not really open.

It was suggested earlier that the focus of community education was particularly affected by changing government policy and this was very clear when in 2007 a new set of national priorities to which CLD would need to respond were identified. The Scottish Government established a Concordat with the Convention of Scottish Local Authorities (COSLA) to deliver its overarching strategy through the setting of key strategic approaches, priorities and outcomes that were agreed with each local authority (Scottish Government, 2007a: part 8). In 2008 COSLA and the Scottish Government issued a statement to show how CLD was delivering change to individuals, groups and communities and identified that it made important contributions to the following outcomes:

> Outcome 3—We are better educated, more skilled and more successful...

> Outcome 4—Our young people are successful learners, confident individuals, effective contributors and responsible citizens.

> Outcome 5—Our children have the best start in life and are ready to succeed.

> Outcome 8—We have improved the life chances for children, young people and families at risk.

> Outcome 11—We have strong, resilient and supportive communities where people take responsibility for their own actions and how they affect others. (COSLA and Scottish Government, 2008: 5)

It is clear from these outcomes that there has been a move from the grand claims made about the efficacy of community education from its advocates to extraordinary expectations about what this small workforce could achieve from central and local governments. However, because CLD was non-statutory provision and the funding for it could easily be reduced, its advocates were anxious to demonstrate its relevance to the current government priorities. This guidance was therefore designed to remind local authorities of its importance. This was particularly necessary because up to this point much of the funding for adult literacy and numeracy (ALN) provision had been 'ring-fenced', with local authorities obliged to spend a particular proportion of their budgets on this aspect of

CLD. However, following the Concordat it was up to the local authorities to decide how they wanted to spend their funding and so the 2008 guidance was framed as a plea rather than a requirement:

> We urge local decision-makers to consider the potential contribu-
> tion of CLD ... delivery to achieving nationally and locally agreed
> outcomes, particularly for those who can benefit most. (COSLA and
> Scottish Government, 2008: 4)

A small concession to supporting the profession was a commitment to invest in continuing professional development (CPD) for the workforce. A Short Life Task Group (SLTG) argued that: 'the consistent availability of a workforce with community learning and development skills is now necessary for the delivery of policy objectives' (Scottish Executive, 2006: 11). Again, the emphasis was on policy requirements determined from the top down rather than on the needs of the workforce. Shortly after this, research was commissioned to see what CPD was available for the workforce. The researchers found that there was limited availability of formal CPD and that support for all forms of staff development was concentrated on the most experienced staff rather than early career staff (Tett *et al.*, 2007). This led to the issuing of a 'position statement' in 2008 (Scottish Government, 2008a) that suggested that CPD was necessary to raise the skills of the CLD workforce through building capacity, and funding was set aside to make this happen. Another recommendation for the improvement of the quality of CLD service delivery led to the setting up of a Standard's Council for Community Learning and Development for Scotland in 2009. The purpose of the Standards Council included the development of CPD and training opportunities and the professional approvals structure for qualifications, courses and development opportunities (Standards Council for CLD, 2009a, 2009b).

In one sense then community education/CLD had moved to mainstream provision since it was now identified as a major contributor to the government's strategic priorities but, at the same time, its practices were more constrained because the focus on outcomes and other inspection regimes meant that there was less space for negotiation with communities about their priorities. For example, the outcome 'supporting productive networks and relationships' (Communities Scotland and Scottish Executive, 2007: 18) could be achieved in a collaborative way that responds to the ideas of a particular community. Alternatively, what is identified as 'productive' could be imposed and reinterpreted in ways that would make people more compliant with current policies. Similarly, although the opportunity for CPD was to be welcomed, the Scottish Government had identified in advance the priorities that it should be focused on. This was yet another example of a policy-led, top-down approach to work that should instead have been responsive to communities.

Problems and possibilities

This short history of the government policies that have shaped the focus of community education/CLD has demonstrated that there has been a continuing debate about how the purpose, role and methodology of the work is conceptualised. Although the focus has generally been on education within and for communities, policies operate with different implicit models of society and 'community' and therefore different assumptions about what is regarded as 'good' practice. These models have been broadly characterised as 'universal', 'reformist' and 'radical' (Martin, 1987). Under the *universal* model it is assumed that there are shared values and a working consensus with a basic harmony of interests and so the community educator's role is to make universal non-selective provision for all ages and groups. The *reformist* model, on the other hand, assumes that there is a plurality of interests with inter-group competition for resources and so selective intervention is made in order to assist disadvantaged people and socially excluded areas. This model leads to a community education that has a more top-down approach that is concerned to solve the problems that impact on the quality of life for people but is not committed to challenging dominant ways of thinking. Finally, the *radical* model assumes that interests are in conflict because existing structures create inequality and powerlessness. In this model the community educator's intervention is based on 'developing with local people political education and social action focused on concrete issues and concerns in the community' (Martin, 1987: 25). Practice grows out of the social and political experiences of people in communities and attempts to forge a direct link between education and social action.

Underpinning all three models is an interest in the role of education and learning in improving social and economic conditions, although the type of provision and the focus for intervention will vary depending on the particular ideology of practice. As can be seen from the various policy documents explored in this chapter, much of the focus of community education has been within the reformist tradition, with the role of combating 'disadvantage' in particular geographical areas to the fore. There is also a strong, but numerically small, movement amongst practitioners who operate under the radical model and who are mainly located in the voluntary sector where there is often more scope for negotiating the agenda with communities. From this perspective the community educator is an agent of social change, who does not separate the process of learning from the intentions of teaching. This tradition has always stood for purposeful educational intervention in the interests of social, economic and political change: change towards more justice, equality and democracy.

From Carnegie (SED, 1977) through to 'WALT' (Communities Scotland and Scottish Executive, 2004) and the National Performance Framework (Communities Scotland and Scottish Executive, 2007) community education has been expected to achieve major change in areas that have been defined as problems by the state. Generally it has been assumed that these changes will be achieved without an increase in resources but through a refocused targeting on the groups or issues that are seen as priorities at that particular time. The problems identified are generally seen as located in geographical communities. This causes additional problems for community educators when the boundaries drawn around particular areas create a community predefined by policymakers, whereas the people living in these spaces may feel that they have little in common. Recently, this targeting of resources has taken a different form whereby the work of community education has been seen as an approach that can be shared and used by other professions such as those working in health or housing (Communities Scotland and Scottish Executive, 2004: 7). This perspective underplays the value of the important body of knowledge, skills and understanding that have been developed through professional training and experience over time by community educators. It also causes difficulties for other professionals who do not understand how to involve communities appropriately.

This also raises issues for both pre-qualifying and continuing professional development (CPD) for community educators. Such education has to take account of the complex, unique, unstable and value-conflict-laden world of the community educator. In these situations problems have to be constructed out of uncertain and confusing situations where the key task is what Schon (1983) has called 'problem setting'. This is the dynamic process in a practice situation by which the decisions to be made, the ends to be achieved and the means of achieving these ends are determined. Where practice situations are uncertain, where ends are not always known, then the selection of the best methodology

cannot be based on only one 'correct' way of doing things. Community educators therefore need space to reflect on their experience and plan for future
action with the people they are working with, but there has been very limited
availability of CPD and, unlike similar professions such as school teaching, no
requirement for regular professional updating. Although the establishment of
the Standards Council for CLD has made some difference in this area, a research
report on the experiences of early and mid-career practitioners in CLD (Tett *et
al.*, 2007) found that opportunities to reflect on their learning in order to develop
their expertise was limited. The research found that practitioners had a 'willingness to engage in learning and a commitment to use the resources that were available to them [but] their experience of the intensification of work and the lack of
time for reflection meant that this was not an easy task' (Tett *et al.*, 2007: 40).

Because policy for community educators is often generated from above in
order to solve current problems rather than from below in response to needs,
workers face dilemmas about the focus of their practice. They have to strike a
balance between the demands of policy and the interests of communities in
ways that are not easily resolvable. This can lead to a focus solely on local issues
at the expense of a broader analysis of their underlying causes. In addition there
is an assumption that the people within a community are all the same and thus
that there is a single set of solutions to their problems. Often, however, people
have ended up living in a geographical 'community' that was created by plan-
ners and politicians in the first place and is therefore unnatural and inorganic.
Such created communities are often used to cover up the pre-existing fault
lines of economic decline and fragmentation. When policy-makers require a
focus on 'disadvantage' and 'exclusion' then education can be seen mainly as a
vehicle for rebinding individuals back into society. From this perspective, community education's main role is to improve skills and help people to become
more employable rather than acting as a force to question and change unequal
social and economic structures. It also means that the interest of the state is in
'deploying *community as policy* to manage and regulate people in communities'
(Martin, 2003: 271), rather than viewing community as a relational concept,
'which articulates the shared experiences of groups, or collectivities, of people'
(Martin, 2003: 272).

Another problem for community education has been a lack of a clear bound-
ary around the discipline that would define the limits of the work it is expected
to undertake. This has led to the making of both unrealistic claims as to what it

can achieve on the part of its advocates and unrealistic expectations on the part of its funders. One reason for this is that, unlike school or university education, there is no middle-class lobby demanding that community education services are properly funded and developed. Nor is there a statutory legislative base that ensures at least a minimum ratio of professionals to populations. Indeed, given the values that some community educators espouse, of being on the side of people who are socially excluded, they may find themselves in the position of opposing their own funders, for example, by helping people to take action about the poor quality of their environment rather than just 'coping' with it. In addition, a focus on the least advantaged groups of the population coupled with a desire to make sure that the participants, rather than the professionals, get the credit for positive changes has resulted in community educators keeping a low profile about the profession's achievements. This in turn has led some policy-makers to blame community educators for their lack of skills in bringing about transformations in individuals or communities. However, the difficult task of changing people and places is not one that can be carried out by education alone. As can be seen by the quotation opening this chapter, 'making a reality of educational opportunity for all' is a goal that has eluded Scottish society for a long time.

As community education takes place mainly in informal contexts outside of institutions and is therefore concerned primarily with the local issues that arise through negotiation with communities it is more difficult to pin down and define. It lacks a grand narrative that encompasses all its work because it depends on the local context and requires a knowledge and understanding of those particular communities and an ability to build and maintain relationships with individuals and groups. This responsiveness also makes it difficult to measure its long-term impact on people's lives as has been acknowledged to some extent by government documents (e.g. Communities Scotland and Scottish Government, 2007). Using the easy head count of participants can mean that community educators try to justify their work by the numbers of people participating. This may not be central to their purpose of trying to engage the most hard-to-reach groups on terms that make sense to them. Part of this problem lies in the negotiations around creating an educational curriculum, where it comes from, whom it serves and what it implies for the community educator's role. Building a curriculum with people is more time consuming and risky than providing a menu of choices from which participants take their pick. However, typical outcome-focused performance measures mean that a preset curriculum is easier to justify and implement. This focus on measurable achievement also leads to a tendency to go for quick-fix solutions that might alleviate the problem in the short term but do not deal with the underlying causes. Rather, responding to communities requires the recognition that the identification of issues involves a long-term process of dialogue and negotiation between community educators and prospective learners. 'As such it provides a clear rationale for reaching out to communities beyond educational institutions and for moving beyond conventional constructions of knowledge' (Johnston, 2000: 15). Community education is a difficult but important task that can make a real difference to the lives of people but is not easy to measure and assess when the focus is on auditing outcomes.

Conclusion

This chapter has provided a short history of community education in Scotland to illustrate the impact of policy on practice. Recently, the Government has identified the key role for community education as addressing the learning needs of disadvantaged individuals and communities. However, whilst it has been suggested that education that is rooted in the interests and experience of ordinary people can contribute to a more inclusive and democratic society, it has also been shown how difficult this task is, especially when educators must react to policy generated 'from above'. Community educators have the potential to respond in a variety of ways to policies and it is important that they are clear about their purpose in intervening in communities. Community education's distinctive epistemology and methodology, that uses the lived experience of people in communities to build the learning curriculum, may simply reinforce the status quo if workers are not self-critical about the implementation of their practice.

Because of the importance of engaging critically with the political context, the next chapter will explore the policy area of lifelong learning in Europe and the UK. The focus will be on how this has been conceptualised and what the implications are for community educators to challenge the narrower definitions in order to find spaces for action.

Chapter 3

Lifelong Learning and Community Education

We should no longer assiduously acquire knowledge once and for all, but learn how to build up a continually evolving body of knowledge all through life—'learn to be'. (Fauré *et al.*, 1972: vi).

According to one estimate, the mismatches between the supply and demand of labour cost the European Union 100 billion Euro each year. Therefore, more needs to be done to implement lifelong learning. We need to raise the levels of investment in human resources. (Van der Pas, 2001: 12)

Introduction

The Scottish Parliament has placed education at the heart of its policies and identified community education as having a key role in addressing the learning needs of individuals and communities through the promotion of lifelong learning. This chapter traces the rise of lifelong learning up the policy agenda, identifies the underlying assumptions that are made and the implications of these for community educators. The importance of this task is illustrated by the above quotations that are posing very different conceptualisations of the purpose of lifelong learning. Whereas in the first quotation lifelong learning is seen as an inherent aspect of democratic life and focused on personal growth, in the second (from an EU Commissioner) it is seen as about the formation of human capital and as an investment in economic development. This illustrates that whilst a commitment to lifelong learning brings many opportunities for growth, development and fulfilment, without careful intervention within a social justice framework, it can also serve to reinforce inequalities.

In the past there was a clear distinction made between schooling that was a preparation for adult life and post-school education that was 'either to provide compensation for inadequate or incomplete schooling or with learning that is somehow distinctive of adulthood' (Field and Leicester, 2000: xvi). 'Lifelong Learning', however, cuts across these distinctions to suggest that the learning process spans the whole of one's life. The term is also used widely to blur the boundaries between learning for work (vocational), learning for citizenship (political), learning for personal development (liberal) and learning that encourages participation in education by previously excluded groups (social). Such blurring, however, can mean that rather than all these aspects having equal importance the vocational takes precedence. How lifelong learning and the learning society are conceptualised, then, has major implications for policy.

Lifelong Learning and conceptualisations of the learning society

The individual's capacity for learning across the life-span means that people can learn in many different ways and contexts. If learning is seen as a normal activity for people of all ages then everyone, rather than a limited group, is likely to be effectively engaged in some form of education of their choice. Currently, however, participation in post-school education and training in the UK is a highly classed activity with those from social classes IV and V unlikely to continue their education and those from social classes I and II overrepresented, particularly in Higher Education (see Aldridge and Tuckett, 2008). Since those who leave school with few or no qualifications are unlikely to engage in learning later, it appears that if you do not succeed in the first place then you will not succeed later either. Participation is also highly gendered where men receive a greater share of substantial employer-funded education and training for adults (Aldridge and Tuckett, 2008).

There are many ways in which a learning society and notions of lifelong learning could be conceptualised. For example, Robert Owen suggested that 'any general character, from the worst to best, from the most ignorant to the most enlightened, may be given to any community by application of good education' (Silver, 1965: 61). Owen regarded learning as a fundamental right of all citizens, whatever their age, and saw it as a key way of developing a more equitable society. Today the idea of a learning society has three models about what its key purpose should be: learning for work, learning for citizenship and learning for democracy (Ranson, 1998).

The world of work has been transformed by structural changes including the use of new information technologies, relocation of labour-intensive industries

to low-wage economies, the shift from manufacturing to services, the intensification of international competition and the growth of part-time, intermittent
employment. A view of the learning society that prioritises 'learning for work'
sees its main task as enabling employees to become more adaptable to a greater
variety of occupational tasks. For example, in 2000 the European Union set itself
a new strategic goal 'to become the most competitive and dynamic knowledge-
based economy in the world, capable of sustainable economic growth with more
and better jobs and greater social cohesion' (Lisbon European Council, 2000:
paragraph 5).

The 'learning for citizenship' approach broadens the narrow conception of
the learning society that concentrates only on skills for work. A much more
enriched view of work and wealth creation is argued for as well as the development of vocational skills. This includes the quality of people's social, cultural
and political life where people come together to engage in a shared endeavour.
Moreover, 'rethinking the nature of work cannot be separated from the social and
cultural relations (between the sexes, races and generations) which define who
works and thus the social conditions of economic growth' (Ranson, 1998: 27).

The 'learning for democracy' approach starts from a concern to make sense
of the economic, social and political transformations that have occurred and
to create a learning society that would be at the centre of change. Such change
requires a renewed commitment to learning that leads to a revitalised sense of
democratic and social purpose. From this perspective a learning society would
have at its heart the qualities of:

> being open to new ideas, listening as well as expressing perspectives,
> reflecting on and inquiring into solutions to new dilemmas, co-oper-
> ating in the practice of change and critically reviewing it. (Ranson,
> 1998: 28)

These differing perspectives have major implications for the work of community educators. Community education can offer an integrated structure for
the promotion of lifelong learning that takes positive action to enable excluded
people and communities to participate in education and training. However, the
opportunities that there are for community educators to promote a learning
society that is for everyone, and does not waste the creativity and knowledge of
many of its citizens, are constrained by the way in which the learning society is
conceptualised. The next part of this chapter examines some of the European,

UK and Scottish policies on lifelong learning in order to identify how these ideas might be developed in ways that would promote a more inclusive society.

Lifelong learning policies

Policies about lifelong learning were first developed in Europe and the UK in the early 1990s. Although there had been a number of policy documents produced by the Organization for Economic Cooperation and Development (OECD) and the United Nations Educational, Scientific, and Cultural Organization (UNESCO) in the 1970s (e.g. Fauré *et al.*, 1972) the idea of lifelong learning only entered the mainstream political vocabulary when the concept was adopted by the European Union (EU) as a key priority. Since the Treaty of Rome the EU had some legal competence in vocational training, but the Maastricht Treaty (1992) gave it legal competence in the education policies of the Member States. This meant it was able to pursue two of its prime objectives of achieving economic and social cohesion and shifting attitudes to both education and training through a focus on lifelong learning (see Field, 2000). These policies became fully operationalised in 1996 when this was declared as the 'European Year of Lifelong Learning', and have been taken up and developed by UK and Scottish governments since.

Policies, as Ball (1990: 22) has argued, are 'statements about practice—the ways things could or should be—which are derived from statements about the world'. What is seen as legitimate in terms of policy and practice privileges certain visions and interests which embody claims to speak with authority in ways that shut out alternatives. A particular conception of what the problem is, and consequently how it is to be solved, becomes dominant and that makes it difficult to see that there are alternatives. So if the problem facing governments is conceptualised as being about employment and training then solutions that prioritise the development of vocational skills follow. If governments see their main task as responding to an economic and employment climate where mobility and short-term contracts have become the norm, with the concomitant need to constantly update knowledge and skills, then they will prioritise learning for work. This leads to a debate that emphasises the economic importance of knowledge and suggests that the 'information and knowledge based revolution of the twenty-first century [will be based] on investment in the intellect and creativity of people' (DfEE, 1998: 9).

However, although the conception of lifelong learning and the learning society as evidenced through these policies may be limited to learning for work, the potential exists for those who are committed to a social justice agenda to interpret the policies more radically. One particular issue has been the prevailing orthodoxy that privileges the view that education must be modernised and become more response to the needs of employers. From this perspective education becomes the mere instrument of the economy. As a former British Prime Minister put it 'Education is the best economic policy we have' (Blair, 1998: 9). Such a view of society denigrates the values of caring and mutual support and values the economic over the social. It also excludes those people who are not part of the 'normal' labour market, such as retired people or those who are caring for young children or those with disabilities that prevent them from working.

In the following section some of the key EU, UK and Scottish policy documents on lifelong learning are examined in order to explore how the policy debate has been constrained through the imposition of particular political discourses.

A European Union Perspective

At EU level the term 'lifelong learning' first appeared in the 1994 Commission of the European Communities (CEC) paper *Growth, Competitiveness, Employment: The Challenges and Ways Forward into the 21st Century'* (CEC, 1994). As the title suggests, the paper was primarily concerned with laying out a formula for economic success within the Union. However, within the introduction, the paper recognises 'lifelong education and training' as key to job retention and economic prosperity. It went on to say:

> Our countries' education and training systems are faced with major difficulties ... [that] are rooted in social ills [such as] the breakdown of the family and the demotivation bred by unemployment. Preparation for life in tomorrow's world cannot be satisfied by once-and-for-all acquisition of knowledge and know how ... All measures must therefore necessarily be based on the concept of developing, generalising and systematising lifelong learning and continuous training. (CEC, 1994: 16, 146)

These paragraphs enshrine many of the key concepts underpinning the European paradigm of lifelong learning. The diagnosis of the problem was that the EU faced the threats and opportunities of globalisation, information technology and the application of science but these could be best dealt with by pooling some of their sovereignty and resources in education and training (see Field, 2000). In order to achieve this Member States were asked to develop policies that met the education and training needs created by long-term unemployment. The paper suggested that this would be most effectively achieved if the delivery mechanisms used were increasingly flexible and if the management of education systems were increasingly decentralised. This view emphasises the value of competitiveness between education and training institutions where decentralised institutions compete with each other to provide the best services. It also values the ability of the intending participant to choose from amongst a range of providers and from different kinds of provision. With such a strong focus on the providers of learning little attention is given to learners and the circumstances that affect their learning. This means that the willingness and ability to participate in continuing education and training is treated unproblematically and it is assumed that, if the supply is there, then demand will follow.

In terms of society and its social cohesion the paper provides an unreflective and somewhat pathological view of 'the family' that has apparently 'broken down'. The consequences of this breakdown are not carefully explored but there is a strong implication that reforming the family, rather than other aspects of society, can alleviate the range of social ills that beset society, such as delinquency, vandalism and child abuse. In this analysis there is an implicit separation of the problems presented by individuals from the social and political order that created the problems and a blaming of women for not prioritising their families' needs. In many ways this approach mirrors that popularised by Etzioni (1993: 61) whose argument was that the decline of the two-parent family lies at the heart of the problems of Western society because both parents are necessary to provide mutually supportive educational involvement if children are to learn effectively.

The stated aim of a second Commission paper, *Teaching and Learning Towards the Learning Society* (CEC, 1995), was to address what were perceived as 'factors of upheaval' affecting Member States. These were identified as the impact of the information society, the impact of internationalisation as it affects job creation, and the impact of the scientific and technical worlds. These were similar to those identified in 1994 but this paper also prioritised education and training concerned with citizenship, personal fulfilment and the tackling of exclusion. This was an important development but the analysis of social exclusion was of a process that happened once and for all. Social exclusion was not seen as a cumulative process that could be compounded by the new emphasis that was placed on having knowledge when those who are deemed unskilled become further marginalised. Just as income inequality polarises the poor from the rich, so the generalisation of lifelong learning could increase the isolation of non-participants from the world of the 'knowledge rich'.

A third Commission paper, *Learning for Active Citizenship*, was published in 1998. It suggested:

> In a high-technology knowledge society ... learners must become proactive and more autonomous, prepared to renew their knowledge continuously and to respond constructively to changing constellations of problems and contexts. (CEC, 1998: 9)

Here the emphasis was on the learner becoming proactive and acquiring the skills and habits of self-regulation and self-monitoring. Learners were seen as individuals, separated from society as a whole, so if they failed to participate in the new learning opportunities they could be blamed for not making the most of the chances they were given. These assumptions become mechanisms for legitimating inequalities that 'may themselves be arising partly from the general acceptance of the idea and practice of lifelong learning' (Field, 2000:104).

In October 2000 the Commission issued a working paper entitled *A Memorandum on Lifelong Learning* (CEC, 2000). In it they stated that there were 'two equally important aims for lifelong learning: promoting active citizenship and promoting employability'. They continued by arguing that 'both employability and active citizenship are dependent on having adequate and up-to-date knowledge and skills to take part in and make a contribution to economic and social life' (CEC, 2000: 5). Although this paper widened the reasons for participating in learning to include social life there was an absence of other purposes such as personal or community development and the emphasis was still on employability.

A principal theme of the period since 2000 has been the development of 'benchmarks' and 'indicators' that will enable the EU to measure and assess progress in lifelong learning (and education and training) on a consistent basis across the Member States (see Holford *et al.*, 2008). As was discussed in Chapter 2, this was part of a common emphasis on measuring performance and outputs rather than inputs. The indicators constructed included 'spending on human resources' and 'investment in the knowledge-based economy' (CEC, 2004: 10). However, the difficulty of reaching the overarching goal of 'becoming the most competitive and dynamic knowledge-based economy in the world ... with more and better jobs and greater social inclusion' was acknowledged as 'immense' in the 2005 Report from the Commission (CEC, 2005: 12).

In 2006 the EU issued a Communication entitled *Adult Learning: It Is Never Too Late to Learn* (CEC, 2006). The focus was almost exclusively on vocational education and training and the Commission argued that adult learning led to many benefits including employability, reduced welfare expenditure, better civic participation but suggested that it 'has not always gained the recognition it deserves' (CEC, 2006: 3). John Holford and colleagues argue that whilst the lack of a focus in this paper on the knowledge economy 'represents a significant shift in the rhetoric of lifelong learning policy' (Holford *et al.*, 2008: 61) there was little evidence that it represented a major change in direction. Neither was there any acknowledgement that 'adults bring something that derives both from their experience of adult life and from their status as citizens to the educational process' (Jackson, 1995: 187). Participants in education and training seemed to be generally constructed as empty vessels to be filled with knowledge and skills by others that were also able to predefine their needs, with the individual having little input to this process.

UK and Scottish Government perspectives

In December 1995 a consultative document on 'Lifetime Learning' was intro-duced for the first time in the UK. While issues of lifelong learning had been raised in other government policies, this was the first coherent view of govern-ment's vision of lifelong learning. The primary concern was with economic competitiveness and human resource development. However, like its European counterpart, it also recognised the importance of learning in other spheres: 'the presentation and acquisition of knowledge and the ability of individuals to fulfil their personal capacity are vital signs of a free and civilised society' (DfEE 1995: 4). Despite this wider vision, learning was seen as responding to market forces with the major roles and responsibilities ascribed to individuals and a minor role ascribed to government. The document embodied an assumption that it was the responsibility of the individual to engage with the learning society and the underpinning ideas were about pragmatic expediency and market principles rather than any wider egalitarian understanding. This was made even clearer by a Scottish Office document issued in 1997 that stated 'Scotland's future competi-tiveness demands a more highly skilled and adaptable work force. To achieve this we must convince individuals of the relevance of continuing learning' (SOEID, 1997: 5).

In February 1998 the new Labour administration issued a Green Paper *The Learning Age*. It again reiterated the need 'for a well-educated, well-equipped and adaptable labour force' (DfEE, 1998: 3) but added '[learning] helps make ours a civilised society, develops the spiritual side of our lives and promotes active citizenship. It strengthens the family, the neighbourhood and consequently the nation' (DfEE, 1998: 3). Throughout the paper there was an emphasis on partnership, with the government's role 'to help create a framework of opportunities for people to learn [by] sharing responsibility with employers, employees and the community' (DfEE, 1998: 6). This was followed by Opportunity Scotland (Scottish Executive, 1998a) that paralleled the concerns of the DfEE paper. In both these documents, whilst there was a clear shift from the earlier emphasis on the primacy of the market, the obstacles posed by class, poverty, employment status, 'race' and gender were not explored.

When there was a concern about those who were excluded, rather than appealing to social solidarity, there was an emphasis on the threat to the established certainties. Thus the UK government's National Advisory Council on Education and Training Targets (NACETT) warned in 1998 that:

> Social exclusion is expensive, not merely because of the burden that it imposes on the social security system, but also because of the indirect costs that arise from, for example, juvenile delinquency and the greater levels of ill health that poorer members of society suffer. (NACETT, 1998: 13)

These sentiments were paralleled in the document *Skills for Scotland: A Skills Strategy for a Competitive Scotland* (Scottish Executive, 1999). Yet Scottish policy already included a much broader understanding of the importance of inclusion because of its commitment to social justice, as can be seen from the following:

> Those of us who benefit from the opportunities of life in modern Scotland have a duty to seek to extend similar opportunities to those who do not. Social exclusion is unacceptable in human terms; it is also wasteful, costly and carries risks in the long term for our social cohesion and well-being. This Government is determined to take action to tackle exclusion, and to develop policies that will promote a more inclusive, cohesive and ultimately sustainable society. (Scottish Executive, 1998b: 1)

A later policy document, *Life Through Learning; Learning Through Life*, emphasised the personal effects for those that miss out on learning as well as the impact on the economy and suggested that:

> In a modern, forward looking, prosperous Scotland we cannot accept: the opportunity gap between people who achieve their full potential and those that do not; the skills gap between people in work and those who are not—35% of those not in work do not have any qualifications; the productivity gap between Scotland and the leading economies of the world. (Scottish Executive, 2003b: 1)

In contrast to this broad view of what is included in lifelong learning, the six indicators that aimed to measure the success of the strategy focused either on young people with low qualifications or on increasing the level of qualifications in the workforce. In addition, the perceived associations between exclusion and anti-social behaviour and the emphasis on a 'flexible and adaptable workforce' (Scottish Executive, 2003b: 1) made it easy to justify and continue with the compulsory requirement to participate in vocational training under the 'New Deal' regulations. In this initiative, adults who were seen as being 'at risk' required experts to help them deal with their problems 'appropriately' (Scottish Executive, 2000a). Moreover, as John Field (2000: 111) has pointed out: 'the fact that individuals are treated as though they can acquire and understand the implications of new information about their well-being becomes in turn a *justification* for reducing public services'.

The stress on economic development was even higher in the *Skills for Scotland: A Lifelong Skills Strategy* published in 2007 (Scottish Government, 2007b). This strategy argued:

> A skilled and educated workforce is essential to productivity and sustainable economic growth. Not only are more skilled workers potentially more productive in their own right, but the skill level of the workforce is likely to impact significantly on the effectiveness of capital investment and the ability of employers to adopt innovative work practices. (Scottish Government, 2007b: 13)

Other benefits 'such as social justice, stronger communities and more engaged citizens' (Scottish Government, 2007b: 10) were expected to flow from economic development rather than the other way around. However, it is clear that if economic development is concentrated on the already highly skilled workforce then inequality is likely to be exacerbated as changes in employment patterns will lead to differentials in income (see Hudson, 2006).

If the assumptions contained in these policies are to be challenged then it is important to create a framework for critically analysing their contradictions so that opportunities for more radical action can be identified. Policies about lifelong learning draw on a number of interrelated fallacies that cumulatively give the impression of a commitment to lifelong learning only in relation to its economic value. However, if these fallacies are separated out and examined it becomes easier to see how those that are committed to a more radical view might challenge them. In order to do this the next section explores each in turn.

Fallacy: education and training are commodities in the market

The policies outlined above put education and training within the marketplace and regard it as a commodity that can be bought and sold like any other good. From this perspective failures in education are assumed to be because the 'producers' of education and training have taken over and pursue their own purposes at the expense of the needs of the 'consumers' of the service. Marketisation and the commodification of public services are thus portrayed as mechanisms that, through the promotion of competition, lead to greater efficiency and increased consumer control. The overt claim is that such policies will bring about an improvement in the quality of educational provision by creating a system in which high quality provision is financially rewarded. However, the covert aim is to undermine the power of those professionals who appear to stand in the way of competition.

There is little empirical evidence, however, to suggest that removal of the power of professionals and the placing of education and training within a market context does improve efficiency or user control. For example, the incorporation of Further Education Colleges, which increased competition and discouraged partnership, led to fewer opportunities for socio-economically excluded individuals and communities rather than more (see Tett and Ducklin, 1995). This research showed that Colleges became less responsive to the education and training opportunities that were asked for by marginalised communities because these opportunities were expensive to provide. Instead, Colleges were more likely to present a menu of existing courses from which learners were expected to pick. Rather than empowering consumers, a market-driven system perpetuates inequalities because, as Stewart Ranson suggests:

> The market elides, but reproduces, the inequalities that consumers
> bring to the market place. Under the guise of neutrality, the institution
> of the market actively confirms and reinforces the pre-existing social
> class order of wealth and privilege. (Ranson, 1994: 95–6)

In a class, gender and 'race'-divided society this process of 'marketisation'
means that 'cultures which give primacy to the values of community and locality' lose out in the 'scramble for educational opportunity based on individual
opportunity and choice' (Bowe *et al.*, 1992: 14). This is because they do not have
the financial and cultural capital to be 'active and strategic' choosers. For those
marginalised by poverty or geography, their choice will be limited by the lack
of accessible provision; for those marginalised by cultural difference, excluded
from current systems, it will be their lack of knowledge and understanding of
the system itself that disadvantages them. There seems little likelihood that the
market will do anything to improve people's dispositional barriers to learning. As
Keith Jackson (1995: 191) points out, 'education is a form of human exchange,
which, if it is to be effective, requires participants to be creative partners'.

A similar assumption is that within the market context education and training are activities that will enhance the individual's ability to engage only in economic life and through this contribute to 'national culture and quality of life'
(DfEE, 1995: 3). Once the citizen is constructed primarily as a consumer a
very particular and limiting notion of lifelong learning follows. At the centre
of the marketisation model is the idea of self-interested individuals as people
with rights to control both their own selves and their own property free from
coercion and restraint. This characterisation of human beings as by nature pos-
sessively self-interested is encouraged by the market approach. An intrinsically
selfish motivation and competition are assumed because people are not seen as
contributors to the democratic society that includes freedom to constrain individual action for the greater good of the whole community. By making lifelong
learning a *private* good that is considered to be only valuable in relation to the
economic function of lifelong learning, as Gert Biesta (2006: 177) points out, it
becomes increasingly difficult to claim *collective* resources for lifelong learning,
particularly resources for supporting its personal and democratic dimensions.

Fallacy: economic success equals eradication of deprivation and exclusion
Within the policies outlined above, inadequate skill levels within the unemployed population were seen as the causes of poverty and learning was identified

as the way out of this trap. It follows that education and training must be modernised and become more responsive to the needs of employers since otherwise they will not meet the needs of the economy. However, the link between education and training and economic development is complex and there is little evidence that participating in learning will necessarily lead to greater prosperity for all. For example, Levin and Kelley (1997: 27), in their review of research in the USA, found that 'test scores have never shown a strong connection with either earnings or productivity'. Rather, they found that if education was to be effective for economic development it was crucially dependent on complementary inputs from business and government. These inputs included new investment, new methods of production and of organising work, new technologies, industrial relations based on trust, sufficient customers able to buy high quality services and new managerial approaches.

Those arguments that equate participation in learning with economic success also ignore the sharpening polarisation in income and wealth that can lead to a fundamental split in societies. Indeed, as the Select Committee on Education and Employment (1999) pointed out, 'a side effect of the substantial improvement in overall participation [in education] during the last two decades has been to widen the gap between the educational haves and the have-nots'. Whilst paid work is seen as the best way of averting poverty and social exclusion at the same time, if people are to be treated in relation to their potential contribution to the market economy, then a value is attached to each individual according to that contribution. 'So people with learning difficulties may come to be seen as a poor investment, more expensive to train, less flexible and less employable' (Coffield, 1999: 485). In these ways social exclusion, defined by the CEC (1993) as 'the multiple and changing factors resulting in people being excluded from the normal exchanges, practices and rights of modern society', is intensified rather than reduced.

A final issue relating to the notion of economic success is the impact of globalisation which is generally presented as a twin process of cross-border corporate expansion and intensifying global competition, in which the world's training and manufacturing activities are woven increasingly closer together (Ritzer, 2000). One impact of this has been to see the nation-state as having diminishing powers and so there is little opportunity to intervene except through promoting education and training as a source of sustainable competition. As Frank Coffield (1999: 480) argues, this leads to the assumption that the 'new economic forces unleashed by globalisation and technology are as uncontrollable as natural disasters and so governments have no choice but to introduce policies to "up skill" their workforce'. Such a view forgets that skills are not neutral but are socially constructed by, for example, trade unions negotiating higher pay for those jobs that are held predominantly by male members or employers offering good quality education and training only to their permanent, highly paid employees.

Fallacy: failure is the fault of the individual

This fallacy is intimately related to the preceding two. Given that the market is perceived as fair and equal, then failure to succeed in a market structure cannot be the fault of the system, but rather is rooted in the failings of the individual to engage appropriately. Within the policy frameworks offered for lifelong learning issues such as non-participation, educational under-achievement, lack of knowledge of the range of education and training opportunities, are not perceived as structural failures but rather issues of individual attitude or ability. However, as Jonker (2005, 123) notes, 'at the individual level, schooling can ... saddle one for life with the feeling that one is doomed to fail. Schooling, in other words, is part of the complex process of shaping and reshaping the self.' So many adults do not participate, not because of low motivation but because of powerful constraints that arise from cultural and social class divisions. School creates (or reinforces) sharp divisions in society, by conditioning children to accept different expectations and status patterns according to their academic 'success' or 'failure'. Through the use of imposed standards and selection, the education system traditionally rejects large numbers of the population, many of who subsequently consider themselves as educational failures (see Tett and Maclachlan, 2007). It is hardly surprising that people do not want to engage in a process that is portrayed as 'learn or else' rather than a contribution to human flourishing.

In many ways lifelong learning is regarded as a 'moral obligation and social constraint' (Coffield, 1999: 488) by the state and employers, and legitimates the shifting of the burden of responsibility for education, training and employment onto the individual. In so doing it 'implicitly denies any notion of objective structural problems such as lack of jobs, and the increasing proportion of poorly paid, untrained, routine and insecure jobs' (Darmon *et al.*, 1999: 33). At the same time the term 'employability' also hides the tensions between training workers to meet the short-term needs of employers and the preparation for frequent changes of job for which high-level general education may be more useful.

If, therefore, it is the structure of society that creates inequalities, and education and training are part of that structure, then why should individuals participate in a system in which they know they start at a disadvantage? It is insufficient simply to recognise inequality and strive for greater inclusion; rather, we need to look beyond that to the causes of that inequality. Moreover, if we regard education as being about responding to individual need then no attention is paid to the ways in which these 'needs' are politically constructed and understood (see Maclachlan and Tett, 2006). By individualising the characteristics, such as a lack of basic skills, that justify employers and others treating people differently, the trend towards lifelong learning also helps fragment the excluded and encourages a search for individual solutions. This pattern then gets reproduced through other areas of public life, such as when the welfare state switches its focus from passive support to actively inserting people back into society, the most significant strategy being through training (see Field, 2000: 111). Individuals are then assumed to be able to acquire the skills and knowledge required for them to take active responsibility for their own well-being.

The fallacy that individual failings lie at the heart of either educational failure or economic success creates a convenient scapegoat for structural inequality justified through the workings of the market. This means that the 'learning society' becomes one more way of reproducing and legitimating existing inequalities. However, as Carnoy and Levin (1985: 4) have argued, 'the relationship between education and work is dialectical—composed of a perpetual tension between two dynamics, the imperatives of capital and those of democracy in all its forms'. For far too long the economic imperative has dominated the democratic imperative and so a long struggle lies ahead for those who wish to redress the imbalance.

Fallacy: access to education is fair

Jackie Brine (2006) has pointed out that the discourse of the EU is premised on a two-track approach to the knowledge rich and the knowledge poor where the former are entitled to investment whereas the latter have their learning needs identified by others. She further suggests that this leads to an 'individualised and pathologised learner that is simultaneously constructed as "*at* risk" and "*the* risk"' (Brine, 2006: 656). This discourse also pervades policy documents from the UK and suggests that the state's role is to facilitate the active citizen who should be engaged in securing their own welfare (Holford *et al.*, 2008). These policies in turn also suggest that access to education is fair because it is the individual that has failed to engage in it. However, the education and training that is available to the most disadvantaged is the least well funded and accessible. For example, only 24.72% of those accepted to university in the UK were from the lowest social classes (Reay *et al.*, 2010) but this is the sector with the highest investment per student. Conversely, adult literacies education lies at the other end of the investment structure and, in addition, this provision is highly vulnerable to cuts when local authority budgets are reduced.

Another way in which access to education is unfair is because those who make decisions about the opportunities that are available are drawn from a narrow group. One effect of this class, gender and 'race' imbalance is that facilities, such as family-friendly services or opportunities that are geographically and culturally accessible that could increase participation and study opportunities for everyone, are seldom prioritised. Privileging vocational and work-based education and training has tended to benefit men more that women partly because of women's predominance in part-time work where the majority are responsible for paying their own fees for learning (Aldridge and Tuckett, 2008).

In addition, an emphasis on new technologies as a way of advancing learning opportunities risks exacerbating social and gender divisions resulting in a 'society divided between the information-rich and the information-poor' (Fryer, 1997: 21). Governments (DfES, 2005; Scottish Executive, 2003b) have put particular emphasis on the use of new technology to deliver learning. They have not shown, however, how the classed and gendered differences in access to, and familiarity with, these technologies are to be overcome. The classed, gendered and 'raced' nature of participation in education and training is often ignored and instead 'equal opportunities' policies based on a meritocratic model are implemented. This model ignores the process whereby opportunities are defined, interpreted and applied by those already in positions of power, which means that lifelong learning becomes one more way of reinforcing the status quo. What is necessary is a 'problematising' approach (see Freire, 1972) that enables oppressed groups to reflect critically on their reality in a way that enables them to alter their social relations. In particular this should address the ways in which:

> Those who failed at school often come to see post-school learning
> of all kinds as irrelevant to their needs and capabilities. Hence not
> only is participation in further, higher and continuing education not

perceived to be a realistic possibility, but also work-based learning is
viewed as unnecessary. (Rees *et al.*, 1997: 1)

Education is not neutral and if people are treated first and foremost in relation
to their potential contribution to the economy then a market value is attached to
each individual according to that contribution. Rather than education becoming
an individual and social force for emancipation it becomes instead an 'investment' on the part of employers and government.

Conclusion

This chapter has suggested that the lifelong learning policies present a powerful policy steer about what should be prioritised precisely because they are so
all encompassing. However, by deconstructing these policies it is possible to
identify a number of paradoxes that throw up contradictions that in turn create
spaces for challenge and alternative action. The possibility of adults construct-
ing their own knowledge and contesting their exclusion is not a priority of these
policies but is a clear possibility for community educators wishing to engage in
dialogues with excluded communities. Knowledge, skills, understanding, curi-
osity and wisdom cannot be kept in separate boxes, depending simply on who
is paying for or providing them. This means that, although much of the funding
that is tied to lifelong learning policy implementation is linked to programmes
that focus on increasing people's employability, there are still spaces for action.
Rather than a narrow conception of learning for the world of work the priority
would be learning for citizenship leading to a revitalised sense of democratic and
social purpose. This would involve, as Jane Thompson argues, 'tackling the urgent
problems and real concerns of people living in the kind of difficult circumstances
that would defeat the most courageous of us' (2001: 11). Community educators
can demonstrate the relevance of lifelong learning to these issues and the next
chapter considers a conception of learning, knowledge and development that
would contribute to a more inclusive democracy. It will discuss how community
education practice can be constructed that focuses on building knowledge and
understanding in ways that lead to greater social justice rather than only prioritising the needs of the economy.

Chapter 4

Learning, Knowledge and Development

The real point, the real practicality [of education], was learning how to change your life. Really useful knowledge is knowledge calculated to make you free. (Johnson, 1988: 21–2)

Introduction

Can learning contribute to a more equal society? There is evidence that if local people are engaged in using their own knowledge then they can develop a capacity for self-determination through 'the construction, interpretation and the re-shaping of their own social identity and social reality' (Cullen, 2001: 64). Such an approach to knowledge recognises that learning is located in social participation and dialogue as well as in the heads of individuals and treats 'teaching and learning not as two distinct activities, but as elements of a single, reciprocal process' (Coffield, 1999: 493). Engaging in learning can contribute to a more robust and active citizenry through enabling people to review more critically and creatively the values and workings of society and developing mutual tolerance of diversity and difference (see Schuller and Watson, 2009: 180). The implications for learning that leads to democratic renewal are that community educators need to think about what would be 'really useful knowledge' to the people with whom they are working. Such knowledge is not value-free, but needs to seek out 'meaningful, practical starting points for curriculum negotiation within a critical structural analysis' (Johnston, 2000: 16). Education's role is to make space for the collective production of knowledge and insight, and then build on what emerges from the experiences of those actively participating in creating it.

This chapter provides two examples of how community educators have worked with adults to build knowledge and understanding that develops from their issues and concerns. The first example focuses on family literacy and the second on health education. These examples have been chosen because they illustrate both how people have been excluded from participation in decision-making processes and also how they might take action against these excluding practices.

Family literacy learning —an example from practice

Constructions of literacy

The common way to think about literacy is to see it as a ladder that people have to climb up. This ladder begins at school and the literacy that adults need is seen as the extension of this process in post-school contexts. The emphasis is, there-fore, on standardising literacy accomplishments through the use of tests, defin-ing what are core skills and pre-specifying uniform learning outcomes. People are ranked from bottom to top with the emphasis on what they cannot do rather than what they can. This leads to a deficit model where those on the bottom rungs are positioned as lacking the skills that they need. The frameworks used to define this ladder are top-down ones, constructed largely in terms of pre-vocational and vocationally relevant literacy requirements. Consequently, they do not recognise the validity of individuals' own definitions, uses and aspir-ations for literacy, with the result that they are 'disempowering' because they are not negotiable or learner-centred and not locally responsive. They define what counts as 'real literacy' and silence everything else. This deficit discourse also gets internalised by individuals and has consequences for how they see them-selves. It undermines their self-esteem and their sense of themselves as learners.

However, the Scottish Government has recognised some of the problems associated with this narrow approach and instead advocated that:

> The aim [of literacy learning] is to access learners' ability to apply their learning to real contexts and to measure the economic, personal and social gains that they make, including their willingness to learn in the future. (Scottish Executive, 2001: 14)

Building on this, the *Adult Literacy and Numeracy Curriculum for Scotland* (Communities Scotland & Scottish Executive, 2005) developed a *social practices* approach to adult literacy and numeracy. This means that rather than seeing liter-acy and numeracy as the decontextualised, mechanical, manipulation of letters, words and figures, literacy is regarded as being located within social, emotional and linguistic contexts:

Literacy and numeracy practices integrate the routines, skills, and understandings, that are organized within specific contexts and also the feelings and values that people have about these activities. If you are worried that you can't do something then you are going to find it more difficult in a public or workplace context than if you were at home in a relaxed situation. (Communities Scotland and Scottish Executive 2005: 3)

These policies and approaches provide opportunities for community educators to base literacy programmes in the life situations of adults and communities in response to issues that are derived from their own knowledge. When the emphasis is put on how adults can and want to use literacy then the focus moves to what people have, rather than what they lack, what motivates them rather than what is seen by others as something they need (see Tett *et al.*, 2006). In addition, where the power to determine the content of the curriculum lies primarily with the student, rather than the provider, then it can be instrumental in challenging these imbalances in deciding what is to be learnt.

Family literacy

The central assumption behind family literacy programmes is that the high degree of correlation between the literacy difficulties of the child and those of the parent means that these two areas should be tackled together. One issue that such programmes are designed to address is the situation whereby teachers make assumptions about building upon home literacy experiences but have little idea of what actually happens there. This means that the literacy history of parents or the differences between home and community practices and those of the school are unexamined. Research suggests that when the range of literacy activities that people already engage in and feel comfortable about are built on, then the culture of the home is positively valued leading to greater self-efficacy for parents (see Tett and Maclachlan, 2007). How parents' self-efficacy can be built up is illustrated by a family literacy project based in an outer-city housing estate in a poor working-class area of a Scottish city. By positively valuing the home and community life of participants it sought to include the literacy practices of everyday life in the curriculum and build on them. The participants in the project were parents of children who attended the primary schools in the area who had said they had literacy problems that they would like to work on in order to help themselves and their children. Less then 10% of the participants were men partly because the courses were held during the day when most fathers were working and partly because almost 50% of the families were headed by lone, female parents. Groups of up to 10 engaged in an educational programme that is detailed below.

Developing the curriculum

When they began the programme, participants were asked to identify the literacy practices that they used at home and in their community lives. The term 'literacy' was widely defined as including the ability to read, write and use numeracy, to handle information, to express ideas and opinions, to make decisions and solve problems (see Scottish Executive, 2001). It was discovered that although the programme participants regularly used a wide range of numeracy, reading and writing practices, they considered them unimportant and not 'real' literacy. Everyday uses included: working out timetables and schedules; budgeting; scanning the TV pages to find out what was on; checking on their horoscopes; understanding a range of signs and symbols in the local environment; writing brief notes for family members; making shopping lists; keeping a note of birthdays and anniversaries and sending cards; texting using their mobile phones; finding information from the internet and sending emails. These existing uses of literacy provided the starting point for the curriculum and so based education in everyday literacy concerns and practices as well as the students' concerns and aspirations about their own and their children's learning and relationships to their teachers. This range of approaches provided a real incentive for learning because it concentrated on what really mattered to the participants.

Negotiating the curriculum in this way was not, however, simply a matter of passing responsibility for its development from the tutor to the student: that would be an abdication of the tutors' critical, interpretative role and specialised skills. Tutors remained responsible for organising a pedagogical context where participants could collectively realise their best potential, where they all become subjects reflecting together *on* the process rather than passive individualised objects *of* the process. From this perspective education was seen as a cooperative activity involving respect and trust. The emphasis on the process of teaching and learning fore-grounded the lived experience of the participants where 'no one teaches another, nor is any one self-taught. People teach each other, mediated by the world' (Freire, 1972: 53). The project tutors valued home and community literacies, the fostering of effective understanding between home and school literacy practices and an emphasis on the wealth of the knowledge that parents contributed to the educational development of their children.

Curriculum approaches were developed that built on a range of strategies that supported, rather than undermined, what parents did. The participants were encouraged to think critically about their own school experiences in a way that avoided simplistic explanations of failure at school. Sharing their negative school learning episodes led to a focus on what made learning difficult. For example, 'I didn't learn because the teachers only paid attention to the bright ones' and 'If you answered a question and got it wrong you were punished so I tried to avoid answering anything', leading to the realisation that 'not learning at school wasn't only my fault'. Positive experiences, such as 'I liked art because the teacher made it fun' or 'Miss Brown took the time to explain the maths I didn't understand so I could catch up with the others', were used to discuss what made learning easier and more positive. In addition, participants were asked to discuss the differences between their own school experiences and those of their children in order to identify changing pedagogical practices. For example, 'The teachers teach them arithmetic in a way I don't understand'; 'Fiona likes going to school which I never did'; 'James' reports tell you what he can do rather than just telling you what he can't do'. Similarly, participants were encouraged to identify and value the things they did with their children that helped them to learn. This included teaching their children local songs and games as well as talking about what had happened that day. The emphasis was on the positive ways in which parents already successfully educated their children through different ways of knowing the world instead of assuming that parents lacked knowledge and skills that the teacher had to impart (see Taylor and Dorsey-Gaines, 1988). So the teaching was based on a group process, where the tutor and students learnt together, beginning with the concrete experience of the participants, leading to reflection on that experience in order to affect positive change.

Using the literacy practices of everyday life

The project also asked students kept a log of their own reading and writing practices and to interview other people in their families about their roles as readers and writers. This showed that the students regularly used a range of oral communication, reading and writing practices but they had not considered them to be important. These included adult–child conversations, listening to family stories and taking part in everyday tasks such as housework that research shows all help children to learn by fostering their attention, developing their thinking and flexibility and using narratives to describe events (Rogoff, 2003). Recognising and working on actual literacy practices provided an appropriate starting point for the curriculum because it grounded educational intervention in the problems of everyday life. This included challenging assumptions about the homogeneity of reading and writing practices since the wide variation in the group's experiences and the influence of gender, ethnicity and class on what was considered 'normal' was revealed through their discussions. For example, Mandy found that her telling of the traditional stories from her 'Traveller' culture, where the whole extended family would gather around to tell ghost stories, was unusual and meant that she and her children had a much better memory for stories than many other people. On the other hand, Jimmy discovered the gendered nature of his practices since it was his wife who remembered to send birthday cards whereas he was expected to deal with more formal writing such as paying the bills. As well as this, a critical examination of the presumptions about family life that were contained in their children's reading books revealed assumptions about nuclear family roles that were at odds with many of the participants' own experiences. The next stage of this part of the project was for the participants to create, with the help of the computers, stories for their children that reflected their own lives. Access to good word-processing and drawing packages enabled attractive texts to be produced that were authentic reflections of the relevant issues in their own families and communities.

The project staff also focused on developing critical language awareness through enabling learners to see language and the reading of texts as problematic (see Wallace, 1992). This involved, for example, collecting texts that the participants came across in everyday use from a range of genres (advertisements, newspapers, letters from school, bills, cereal packets, 'junk mail', emails and family photograph albums) to work on as a group. They were asked to identify: to whom the text was primarily addressed; who produced it; why it was interesting and what message the producer was trying to get across so that they could see that all writing was created for particular purposes. Such decoding challenged the participants' taken-for-granted assumptions that there was just one form of writing and helped them to see that the writing that they created could vary in form too. Student-led investigations, which involved taking Polaroid photographs of a range of public writing including graffiti, public notices, shop signs, posters, and then coming together to decode these pictures, enabled discussion to take place about the concerns in the community and the messages that were presented to them. Both these approaches enabled the participants to see the ways in which literacy is constructed in different contexts and for different purposes and led to lively discussions. Two examples were the prevalence of racism in the community as revealed through graffiti on the walls of the houses and how particular family life-styles, including having two parents, were assumed by the manufacturers of breakfast cereals. These thematic investigations, or codifications, were based on the ideas of Paolo Freire (1972) and were designed to help the parents to step back from the immediacy of daily life and observe it from a distance so that they could reflect on their social situation and their own place within it.

Sometimes the materials produced by the students were used to create a group poem around the theme of the discussion so that individual contributions led to a collective, cooperative outcome. On other occasions, the theme generated letters of complaint to the appropriate authorities, for example, in relation to the removal of racist graffiti. The general approach of the project was to link reading with writing and talking so that these three important facets of literacy could be brought together. Oral language, especially in relation to rhymes, story-telling and word games, was used to highlight the importance of using the language of the home and community in other contexts including the school. This approach involved the recognition that some people are at a disadvantage because of the ways in which a particular literacy is used in dominant institutions. 'The culture children learn as they grow up is, in fact, "ways of taking" meaning from the environment around them' (Heath, 1983: 49) and not a 'natural' way of behaving. The social practices of the school and other institutions, and the language and literacy they reinforce, were made visible to show that they represented a selection from a wider range of possibilities, none of which was neutral. These practices then became a critical resource for learning and literacy.

Another important aspect of the project was the use of authentic assessment situated in real life contexts, which was done *with*, not *to*, participants. The ability to make changes in their practices and take action was used to assess their progress rather than standardised tests. This process-oriented focus involved students developing a 'portfolio' of examples of their literacy work as evidence of what they had learnt. Portfolios included the titles of books that participants had read with their children; stories that they had created about their own family life;

letters and emails written to friends and families; diaries; examples of reading and writing from a variety of contexts including church, neighbourhood meetings, work; as well as photographs of writing that had interested them. This type of assessment helped the students to reflect both on what they had learned and also how they learned and gave them opportunities to test out their newly acquired skills, knowledge and understanding. Reflection was enhanced when the portfolio was brought along to the group and formed part of a 'show and tell' session that could also be shared with the children. Assessment was based on the extent to which students had been able to change their literacy practices from their own baselines—the distance that they had travelled. This type of assessment also allowed changes in relationships, particularly with their children and the school, to be recorded. This was a very different approach from the way in which people's learning is normally assessed, through the use of standardised outcome-based methods, and was empowering to both students and tutors. For students it enabled them to take responsibility for their own learning and have an equal say in the direction it should take based on their own goals. For tutors it provided feedback on the programme design, content and delivery and the strengths and weaknesses of their approaches.

By taking a critical approach to speaking, reading and writing practices the participants in this project were enabled to see that there are a variety of literacies rather than just the one used by the school. This, in turn, helped to challenge the deficit views of the culture of the home and the community that had been internalised by many parents. As they gained confidence in their own literacy practices they were able to interact on a more equal basis with the school's staff so that they were involved more directly in their children's education. This required the development of a greater understanding by teachers of what parents needed to know about school practices that was partly achieved through joint training sessions with the family literacy project and school staff. The other aspect of confidence building was through helping parents be in a better position to know what to ask the school about their children's progress that took account of the culture of the local community. Parents learnt by sharing and valuing experiences as well as by suggestions and ideas introduced by the tutor.

Working together

This project also showed the value of people working together as a group. Good relationships between and amongst tutors and students created an atmosphere of trust where support, encouragement and constructive feedback helped people to take risks. Being in a positive environment gave people the 'scaffolding' (see Vygotsky, 1986) to go that little bit further with their learning and to stretch their understanding beyond what they currently knew. The project also demonstrated the importance of the emotional and social dimensions of learning and how working together helped the parents to see learning as both possible and valuable. For example, 'Being part of the group has helped me to keep going even when things were really difficult at home' and 'The others knew I didn't like writing on the flip-chart because my spelling isn't good but with their encouragement I did it and after that I felt really proud of myself'. This approach in turn enabled the parents to become more autonomous in their learning and develop the ability to use their own judgement regarding the quality of their work. For example, 'The first version of my letter to the council about the graffiti was all muddled up so I rewrote it four times before I was satisfied it said what I wanted' and 'I was asked to do a reading by my Church so I got the other parents to listen to me and tell me how it sounded and gradually learned that I had to say it really slowly if people were going to understand me.' Parents and tutors together formed a community of practice that acted as a 'locus of engagement in action, interpersonal relations, shared knowledge, and negotiation [that are] mediated by the communities in which their meanings are negotiated in practice' (Wenger, 1998: 85). This approach to the assessment of learning also enabled some of the parents to move on to more formal provision and the project tutors developed relationships with other providers so that individuals could easily go to the local Further Education College and take courses that led to accreditation if they wished.

Another aspect of working together was that the parents were able to attach meaning and significance to shared experiences and common understandings created out of a variety of contexts and circumstances. For example, parents said:

> Khurshid got to make friends with the other children where before I'd kept her in because I was afraid they would all be racist.
>
> I was the only dad in the group and felt a bit ashamed that I was looking after Kim because my wife can earn more than me. But I've learnt that I'm OK as a dad and that I can learn myself and help Kim with her schoolwork.

As a result of this project people were able to reflect on their experience and add new and different knowledge. It put people back at the heart of learning, as the subjects of learning rather than the objects of educational interventions that were supposed to be good for them. Learning then becomes a shared endeavour between tutors and students, a two-way, rather than a one-way, process (see Thompson, 2001).

Educational development and health—a second example from practice

Health inequalities

The second example from practice focuses on the relationship between educational development and health. A great deal of research has shown that poor health and premature death is caused by the structural factors of inequality and poverty and the ways in which these material conditions cause psychosocial stress in early life (e.g. NHS Health Scotland, 2009; Marmot and Wilkinson, 2006). In Scotland life expectancy for those born in 2001 was predicted to be 74.6 years for men and 79.8 for women in the more affluent areas compared to 69.2 for men and 76.5 for women in the least affluent areas (Macintyre, 2007: 5). These inequalities at birth are exacerbated because universal medical services are used more by advantaged social groups and so are less available to those who are poorer. This is known as the 'inverse care law' (Tudor Hart, 1971) and it operates because more advantaged groups have better access to the resources of time, finance and coping skills than those who are poor. This means that advantaged people are able to avail themselves of help to, for example, give up smoking and can also access preventive services such as immunisation, dental check ups and cervical screening more easily (Macintyre, 2007: 8). The place where people live also has a fundamental impact on the quality and meaning of their day-to-day life and health. These include social relations with people, the physical fabric of the locality and the local geographies of services and facilities. Research shows that, in combination, features of place can be either sustaining or undermining of psychosocial well-being and health (Gattrell et al., 2000: 166).

Participating in education cannot change these structural inequalities but it does have an impact on people's well-being and on their ability to access services (Hammond, 2004; Macintyre, 2007). To illustrate this impact a course is examined called 'Health Issues in the Community' that has involved people from throughout Scotland in investigating their concerns about local health issues. The course provided opportunities for people to express their own views, and to question dominant assumptions and explanations, particularly where they differ from their own experience. It draws on people's lived experience of individual and community health problems to build a curriculum based on the issues that are important to them and their communities. This has involved tutors developing a meaningful relationship with each group so that the design of the programme takes account of the influences that impact on them. Like the literacy project described earlier, this programme focuses on the role that participants' own knowledge and development can play in contributing to change.

The assumption underpinning the course is that damaging social experiences produce ill health and that remedial action needs to be social. This view of health focuses on the socio-economic risk conditions such as poverty, unemployment, pollution, poor housing and power imbalances that cause ill health. It also emphasises that 'people's experiences of health are more about the quality of their emotional and social situation than about their experience of disease or disability' (Labonte, 1997: 9). The perspective taken by the course was that an important way that inequalities in health can be tackled, and social exclusion reduced, is to find ways of strengthening individuals and communities so that they can join together for mutual support.

At the end of each course participants investigated and wrote about a health issue in their community that they believed was important and a selection of their writings has been published in three books edited by Jane Jones (1999a; 1999b; 2001). This section draws on these published writings by using the words of the participants to demonstrate the impact of these health issues and the action they took to bring about change.

Housing and health

Poor housing was one of the major health issues identified by those living in socio-economically excluded communities. As one student put it:

> In my community due to poor housing design and inadequate heating systems families are forced to live with dampness. If they did heat their houses properly they probably would not be able to afford to eat, and are therefore forced to live with dampness in their homes. (Frank, in Jones, 1999b: 8)

High-rise flats are a common feature of socially excluded communities and the isolation this type of housing causes was another factor that led to stress and depression. 'Isolation is a major problem in the flats as you can go for days without seeing anybody' (Cathy, in Jones, 1999b: 9). Animosity between neighbours was also a problem when people were living, quite literally, on top of each other. This was often combined with overcrowding, especially for those with large or extended families.

Participants in the course demonstrated that one way of ending the spiral of despair regarding poor housing and ill health was through community development. This meant that rather than seeing dampness and the noise pollution caused by poor housing as an individual trouble, that must be solved by an individual taking action on his or her own, the reasons behind the problem were examined:

> The way forward was through people coming together to tackle the problem as a public issue rather than a private one. Our strategy was forcing the housing department to address the problem of poor housing and developing effective procedures in dealing with noisy neighbours. (Alan, in Jones, 1999b: 35)

Through the process of developing strategies for tackling the problems and taking their issues to the wider community the group grew in confidence and were able to take well-thought-out solutions to policy-makers. One group involved in the course eventually gained better insulation, cladding, soundproofing and heating for their houses through a long campaign of local and wider action. As one member of the group reported:

> The [better housing] had an instant effect on improving people's health both directly and indirectly by reducing people's stress and anxiety levels. Your home should be a place where you can relax, unwind and escape from the outside world. (Jimmy, in Jones, 1999b: 35)

Contesting official definitions of health

It appears that health professionals' dominance over the definition and analysis of health and illness is still disproportionately influential in health policy and practice (see Carlisle, 2001; Graham, 2000; Macintyre, 2007). It is difficult for policy-makers to recognise the political and social determinants of health, and to make the connections between the psychosocial effects of lack of control over the social and material conditions of people's lives, and poor health. Moreover, there is a pervasive assumption that it is people's individual life styles that need to be changed in order to improve health rather than their social and material conditions. Contesting these official definitions of health was, therefore, a key issue in working with communities on their own health issues. This had a number of implications that are now explored.

If people feel that they are able to take action about their circumstances and recognise that their problems are not their individual responsibility then much can change. For example, one student was angry that the media blamed people for their own poverty and got together with other people to see what they could do. The group talked to community education staff and they helped them to sort out what were the important issues and how to work from there. The student explained:

> Healthy diet was a big issue and it was the priority. The shopping centre was the only place in our town that you could get fresh fruit and vegetables but the prices were way above most people's budgets. We decided to take action first of all about telling people what were healthy foods. Then we went to our local farmer to buy our fruit and vegetables so that we could sell them cheaper, only adding on the cost of petrol. The group sent out leaflets giving information on where to go to buy cheaper fruit and vegetables, the response was staggering. Everyone knows what a healthy diet is but they just can't afford it. (Hetty, in Jones, 2001: 33)

This example illustrated the difficulty that people living in less advantaged areas had in easily accessing a healthy diet where living on a limited income meant that food could not be wasted.

Another challenge for people was to see the potential of effective social action. Poor people often blamed themselves for the burdens that they carried and hid their feelings of guilt and inadequacy away. One aspect of changing this was to challenge the stigma associated with mental health and the medical solutions that were offered. Participants in the course described their worries about going to the doctor with their symptoms and their fears about the impact this would have on their children. For example, one student said, 'It is really frightening to say what you feel. You think, if I tell them that, the bairns [children] will get taken away. You're frightened of being labelled a bad mother' (Joan, in Jones, 1999a: 91).

Moving from an individual solution to one that comes from collective action was the next step in the process of analysis, but this usually needed the intervention of 'skilled helpers' (see Brookfield, 2000). One way in which the 'Health Issues in the Community' course provided such help was to show how apparently private troubles were actually public issues (Mills, 1959). An important aspect of this was to look at the issue of mental health. For example, one student commented on the way in which her own understanding had changed:

> I had been on tranquillisers but I felt so ashamed about it that I hid it from everyone. Then this young woman spoke up about her experience in the discussion group and I realised that lots of women had had the same feelings. You have to learn that it isn't your fault but you need people to talk to about it first. (Laura, in Jones, 1999a: 130)

Working with a community to increase self-determination through collective organisation and action was an important task for the tutors. Building organisations and ensuring that community voices were heard had direct health benefits. For example, another student reported:

> I'm involved with the Stress Centre now that got set up because a group of us thought about what would have helped us more than just getting a prescription. We decided that it was somewhere to go to get some support and someone to talk to, so we met a lot of different people and eventually the Centre was set up. Working there has done a lot for my self-confidence and I know that we can help people. It takes time but it can be done. (Norah, in Jones, 1999a: 133)

The people who participated in this course have involved themselves in action that has enabled them to have their voices listened to about the health issues that are important to them. At the individual level this has raised their self-esteem and confidence as shown above. This in turn has enabled them collectively to have an impact on decision-making and the use and distribution of resources in relation to health. For example, a group of older people gained a chiropody clinic in their community as a result of presenting the results of a local questionnaire about the difficulties there were in accessing the provision in the nearby town (Jones, 2001). Research shows that lack of control over one's own destiny promotes a susceptibility to ill-health for people who live in difficult situations where they do not have adequate resources or supports in their day-to-day lives (see Graham, 2000). This course has demonstrated that by taking action about the health issues that were important to them people have made a real difference to their personal and collective health.

An alternative discourse of learning, knowledge and development

These two examples have shown the importance of listening to local voices and building a curriculum that assumes that people are knowledge-rich rather than deficient. This has implications for community educators' practice since all learning represents the practical articulation of a particular set of values. This means that what is counted as important knowledge needs to be considered as one way in which inequalities of power are reproduced. In a democracy, political representatives, public institutions and services, the activities of those who work for them (e.g. doctors, teachers, welfare workers), community organisations and groups, have to be accountable to the people they represent, or work for. Learning and education should, therefore, contribute towards enabling people to interrogate the claims made and activities done on their behalf and, in turn, encourage them to develop the skill, analysis and confidence to make their own voice heard (Crowther and Tett, 2001: 109). Education should also help people to engage in a wide range of political roles and social relationships that occur outside both the workplace and the marketplace.

Community educators need, through their daily practice, to demonstrate the efficacy of this model of gaining knowledge, skills and understanding that focuses on learning for democratic renewal rather than on increasing economic competitiveness. Seeing the effects of this way of working in action helps policy-makers, and others involved in the delivery of education and training, to under-stand that alternative constructs of learning are effective in enabling individuals and communities to fulfil their social and personal, as well as their economic, needs. The diverse purposes and contradictions of lifelong learning highlighted in Chapter 3 provide challenges and opportunities for community educators and places them in a central position to debate the ideas and how they might be interpreted. This is a position that they should be exploiting, since the ambi-guity of policies provides opportunities to use these spaces to develop a more radical practice. Lifelong learning policies can also offer opportunities for the fostering of active citizenship and social inclusion. For example, the Scottish Executive (2001: 8) has suggested that 'an inclusive society is also a literate society'. Stimulating and supporting education for a more active and inclusive construction of citizenship involves marginalised people recognising that their capacity for learning and generating new knowledge is their key resource.

Lifelong learning and the opportunities it represents can be used as a unifying force, not only between providers but also between different interest groups, in ways that ensure that this process challenges oppression and exclusion. This will involve the nurturing of an education and training system whose function is not to reflect and reproduce existing inequalities in society but rather one that prioritises provision for those whose earlier educational and socio-economic disadvantage should give them a first claim in a genuinely lifelong learning system. Educators can then act as an emancipatory force for change especially if they start:

> from the problems, experiences and social position of excluded majorities, from the position of the working people, women and black people. It means working up these lived experiences and insights until they fashion a real alternative. (Johnson, 1988: 813)

Within this paradigm people's classed, 'raced' and gendered experiences would be seen as an educational resource to be used, rather than a deficiency to be rectified.

Education and learning which is rooted in social interests can represent a resource for people to identify inequalities, probe their origins and begin to challenge them, using skills, information and knowledge in order to achieve and stimulate change. Through this type of learning, the production of knowledge is put back into the hands of people, competing values can be thought about and their relevance for people's lives can be assessed. Clearly, whilst education alone cannot abolish social divisions it can make a contribution to combating them, not least by tackling the ways in which social exclusion is reinforced through the very processes and outcomes of education. People's 'success' or 'failure' in school have a long-lasting effect on how they perceive themselves and are perceived by others. The dominant myth of meritocracy implies that anyone who is brought up properly, who is supported enough by caring parents, who is loved and feels good enough about themselves, will rise above the hardships imposed by poverty, sexism and racism. This myth permeates common-sense understandings of what learning implies because failing to meet the demands of schooling is seen as an individual problem. As Mohanty (1994: 147) points out:

> Education represents both a struggle for meaning and a struggle over power relations. Thus education becomes a central terrain where

power and politics operate out of the lived culture of individuals and groups situated in asymmetrical social and political positions.

Once people and communities are positioned as failures then it becomes difficult to make choices and have their desires fulfilled. However, if they can be helped to challenge individually-based, deficit views of themselves and their communities then a small step has been taken in enabling their voices to be heard.

Conclusion

This chapter has shown that learning and development that builds on experience and emphasises the wealth of people's knowledge, rather than their deficits, is more effective. It is a conceptualisation of learning that is grounded in the life situations of adults leading to the joint development of a curriculum based on the knowledge that people bring from their own family and community contexts. The curriculum should lead to the development of a critical understanding of the social, political and economic factors that shape experience. The challenge for community educators is to capture the positive belief in the power of learning and in the potential of all people that comes from engaging in more democratic decision-making about what is important knowledge. This type of learning society, that has at its heart the qualities of 'co-operating in the practice of change and critically reviewing it' (Ranson, 1998:28), would provide some real choices about what being a citizen means and show how everyone can contribute to democratic processes.

These two case studies have illustrated the importance of responding to the voices of those who are excluded. When people do not have their voices heard their only other option is to exit from participation in decision-making to the detriment of the wider society that then creates policies *for* people rather than *with* them. As Ian Martin argues:

> 'Community education' is about evolving more open, participatory and democratic relationships between educators and their constituencies ... The reciprocal quality of these relationships is crucial: community educators claim to work with people—not for them, let alone on them ... This fundamental element of role redefinition and reversal has wide ranging implications for the nature of educative relationships, the context of learning and the potential for redistribution of educational opportunity. (Martin, 1987: 17)

Faced with a dominant discourse that blames people for the poverty that they suffer it is easy for these feelings of failure to be internalised and so confidence and self-esteem are lost. When people are excluded from participation in decision-making as well as access to employment and material resources then individual action that will change their circumstances becomes almost impossible. Working together on local issues can, however, lead to the development of a political culture that focuses on the fundamentally unequal nature of society rather than people's individual deficits. Emphasising the importance of the redistribution of resources shows that there are alternatives to increasing inequalities. These alternatives will grow out of the local politics that are founded in civil society. Popular participation in these more active forms of politics therefore needs to become central to the process of democratic renewal for communities struggling to change their circumstances (see Crowther, 1999).

This chapter has concentrated on work with adults so the next chapter, by Ian Fyfe, will focus on work with young people and in particular how they can participate in the decision-making that affects their lives.

Chapter 5

Young People and Community Engagement

Ian Fyfe

> When local people are actively engaged in tackling issues within their community, and in helping to realise the community's potential, those people are likely to have an increased interest in and engagement with the affairs of local government and indeed Government across the board. (Scottish Government 2009: 7)

> Young people's engagement in public life holds out some great promises. (Kovacheva 2005: 20)

Introduction

Engaging local people in decision-making is an important focus for the work of community educators. In recent years community engagement has become an essential feature of public service planning, development and delivery. As a result, new opportunities and challenges for practice have emerged around the involvement of local people in shaping services to meet their needs. In this chapter community engagement is discussed as a vehicle for the development of the knowledge, skills and values that support meaningful participation in civic and public life with a focus on young people.

The promotion of community engagement sits alongside a myriad of often-competing policy streams that are targeted at the lives, lifestyles and behaviours of young people. Community educators engaged in youth work practice respond directly to policy through targeted provision and are also involved in projects that enable local young people to evaluate and shape the future direction of policy. Youth work practice has become widely acknowledged as a key provider in the broader sector concerned with education for citizenship. Enabling and empowering young people to become active citizens has been recognised as a legitimate aim of youth services in both the public and voluntary sectors (HMIE, 2003). This has involved raising young people's awareness of their rights and responsibilities and supporting active interest and involvement in the demo-cratic process. Additionally, youth workers have helped young people to develop the skills and confidence required to participate in decision-making within differ-ent aspects of their lives. This chapter undertakes a critical analysis of the goals of community engagement bringing new meaning to existing approaches to youth participation and highlighting some new challenges to youth work practice.

Youth participation as community engagement

Youth participation is not a new area of concern for community educators. Indeed, current emphasis on the relationship between youth work practice and notions of active citizenship in Scotland can be tracked back to the mid-1980s. The publica-tion of the report *Our Tomorrow* by the Scottish Community Education Council (SCEC) (SCEC, 1986) brought to the fore notions of youth participation and an emphasis upon methods of practice concerned with issues in the broader social context of young people's lives. In 1989, the Principal Officers Group within the Scottish Community Education Service encouraged practitioners to recognise that one of their primary functions was the promotion of youth work 'within a community development framework and concerned with the individual's role in society and their active participation in it' (SCEC, 1989: 2). A community devel-opment process was seen as an essential vehicle for supporting young people to achieve their potential as citizens within civil society.

In 1996 a national report—*Agenda for a Generation*—produced by the UK Youth Work Alliance (SCEC, 1996) outlined the positive outcomes of the active participation by young people in youth work provision. The new Labour gov-ernment elected in 1997 proclaimed a commitment to the priorities of Lifelong Learning, Social Inclusion and Active Citizenship (Scottish Office, 1998a) and a similar agenda for change was implemented in England following the pub-lication of the *Crick Report* in 1998 (Advisory Group on Citizenship, 1998). This Report contained the vision for citizenship education and the teaching of democracy in schools, both within and outside the formal curriculum with tan-gible links to the local community. Achieving the goal of active citizenship was supported by an educational curriculum framed around the three goals of social and moral responsibility, community involvement and political literacy (Hall *et. al.*, 2000). Youth work organisations were identified by the *Crick Report* along-side a range of education, training and voluntary organisations as having 'great potential value' as partner agencies in education for citizenship (Advisory Group on Citizenship, 1998: 27). The recommendations also stressed the importance of discussing the notions of citizenship and democracy in relation to issues that the participating young people identified as important in their own lives.

In the wake of the developments in England a national consultation process on education for citizenship was undertaken in Scotland, resulting in the publication of the framework document *Education for Citizenship in Scotland* by Learning and Teaching Scotland (LTS). Within the document citizenship was seen to encompass:

> the specific idea of political participation by members of a democratic state. It also includes the more general notion that citizenship embraces a range of participatory activities, not all overtly political, that affect the welfare of communities ... Citizenship is about making informed choices and decisions, and about taking action, individually and as part of collective processes. (LTS, 2002: 8)

As can be seen, participation is central to this definition. The programme of learning proposed in the framework set out not only the provision of information and knowledge but also the development of the skills required to participate effectively as active citizens. The vision was for 'young people to be active and responsible members of their communities—local, national and global' (LTS, 2002: 3). Emphasis was placed on the value of learning about citizenship through being active.

More recently, notions of participation and active citizenship have been crystallised in the broader policy priorities in Scotland relating to community planning and engagement. Community Education/CLD is at the forefront of these objectives. The publication in 2004 of *Working and Learning Together to Build Stronger Communities* called for CLD practitioners to play 'a more central role in supporting the involvement of communities, including young people, in the community planning process' (Communities Scotland and Scottish Executive, 2004: 3). Among the priorities drawn up for CLD were increasing levels of community involvement to tackle issues of concern, and supporting:

> individuals, groups and communities, including young people, to work with and influence the planning and delivery of services at local and strategic levels. We aim to increase the effect the community has on planning and service-delivery decisions. (Communities Scotland and Scottish Executive, 2004: 8)

Across the Scottish local authorities, Community Planning Partnerships were established to engage local citizens, including young people, in the ongoing monitoring and development of public services. To aid this process the Scottish Executive published *National Standards for Community Engagement* (Communities Scotland, 2005). These were universally endorsed by a wide range of public and voluntary sector organisations. The standards were based on a number of principles that highlighted the importance of equality and diversity, promoting a clear sense of purpose, effective methods of achieving change, building on the skills and knowledge of those involved and a commitment to learning for continuous improvement (Scottish Government, 2008b).

From this document is seems that the active participation of young people is vital in bringing to bear their views on the ongoing development of public services. However, the relationship between young people and the policy objectives is not as straightforward as the documentation reviewed would suggest. The simple terms used to describe the aspirations of community engagement conceal some complex activities in relation to the broader policy discourse. Consequently, this requires further analysis to uncover the contrasting forces at play that drive policies directed at young people.

Youth policy—locating the discourse

The UK has a long-standing legacy of policy initiatives targeted at young people where the deliberate intervention of the state impacts upon their life-spheres in areas such as education, welfare, justice and work. The ongoing development of youth policy is a haphazard journey that drifts between competing political priorities. For Considine, any policy intervention must be understood within the social and economic conditions through which resources are identified and any inherent conflicts arise. He offers the insight that:

> The policies of governments contain and express the conflicts and tensions of contemporary societies. Sometimes they do this well and we see new rights and opportunities being confirmed. At other times these same policies are themselves the embodiment of what needs to be changed. Policy-making is thus a unique institutional environment and a political tool. (Considine, 2005: 1)

The range of policies targeted at the lives and lifestyles of young people tend to reflect these conflicts and tensions. The consequence, according to Dwyer and

Wyn (2001: 56), is an 'uneasy balance' between a concentrated focus upon the perceived problems associated with youth, and assumptions made about what constitutes the 'normal' experience of growth into adulthood. This imbalanced relationship is a common feature of contemporary policy discourse whereby, on the one hand, young people are seen to be a threat to the social stability and the moral fabric of society, and on the other, they are viewed as a future asset that demands our investment.

In Table 5.1, three discrete typologies of youth in contemporary policy provide a guiding framework; summarising the dominant features that underlie the respective policy streams.

Table 5.1 Typologies of Youth in contemporary Policy			
Dominant Policy Discourse	Young people at risk	Young people as or in trouble	Young people as active citizens
Policy Context	Risk Society	Community Safety	Active Civil Society
Focus	Deficit	Deviance	Development
Social Purpose of Intervention	Social Care/ Protection	Social Control/ Prevention	Social Change/ Participation

These representations have been forged around distinct contemporary policy discourse relating to public perceptions of young people: namely, young people deemed to be 'at risk', young peoples' behaviour viewed as troublesome and deviant, and young people profiled as active citizens.

Young people 'at risk' in the community

The notion of risk has become endemic to all spheres of life, and subsequently adopted as a common currency in research and policy formulation concerning young people. Contemporary youth are seen to be navigating through a so-called 'risk society', and in doing so, negotiating their way along transitional pathways shaped by social structures and systems that are unrecognisable to their parents (Furlong and Cartmel, 2007). The systematic restructuring of the youth labour market, restricted access to welfare benefits and a limited choice of suitable and affordable housing has created greater dependency upon families and the state. The result is a protracted journey towards the traditional markers of adulthood.

The dominant public discourse that presents young people to be 'at risk' is all too often preoccupied with issues such as school failure, youth unemployment, levels of homelessness, teenage pregnancy, drug and alcohol misuse and 'childhood' obesity (MacDonald, 1997; Dwyer and Wyn, 2001; Griffin, 2004; Batsleer, 2008). The emerging discourse is supported by the use of alarmist stereotypes in the media, fuelling the promotion of moralistic judgements about the perceived threat that young people pose to social stability. The tendency is to identify these social problems as youth problems, and subsequently particular sections of the generation become labelled as 'problem' youth. Essentially, there is a danger of young people being treated according to how they are defined (White and Wyn, 2004). Also, the broader structural factors impacting on young people are often 'ignored or down-played' (Payne, 2009: 223). The resultant alienation and stigmatisation of young people masks their ability to make a valuable contribution to community life. Rather than embrace their potential role in community engagement, a preoccupation with those young people 'at risk' dictates a targeted policy response; accompanied by specific frameworks for assessment, intervention and management (Hine and Wood, 2009)

Young people 'as trouble'

Closely related to the 'at risk' policy lens is a parallel stream more concerned with the regulation and control of behaviour and movements within the public spaces of their communities; essentially a form of 'spatial apartheid' (Wyn and White, 1997: 139). Increasingly, young people are subjected to closer surveillance and supervision than their adult counterparts and previous generations of youth. During the past two decades we have witnessed in the UK a range of authoritative measures introduced to monitor and control our alleged deviant youth. These have included curfews, electronic tagging and anti-social behaviour orders. The concern over the incidence of juvenile crime has generated both public anxiety and outrage. Young people have long been the subjects of adult unease in relation to their perceived criminal or anti-social activities and as a result they have become objects of moral panic. The media through negative portrayals of their behaviour invariably fuels dominant public perception of the alleged dangerousness of today's youth. These powerful narratives built on combined public fear and intolerance has in actual fact veiled general downward trends in youth-related criminal activity. The net result for young people is 'ever-greater state interventions designed to control their behaviour' (Wood, 2009: 146).

So, the policy terrain has tended to focus on the perceived problems young people present to society, and conversely, those that they face. Although, rather than young people being viewed as a homogeneous group, the intervention of the state is often swayed by the variable perspectives of social class, race, disability and sexuality. For Griffin, the resultant policy discourse is deliberately constructed to match with the specific demographic constructions of young people. Her main contention is that:

> Young people are frequently presented as either actively 'deviant' or passively 'at risk, and sometimes as both simultaneously. In general young men are more likely to be presented as actively 'deviant', especially in aggressive forms, and especially if they are working class and/ or black. Young women, however, are more likely to be constructed passively 'at risk'. (Griffin, 2004: 10)

However, for Barry, the underlying imbalance of attention in current policy and practice is fuelled by perceived tensions in inter-generational relationships, and central to this social phenomenon is the dynamic of power. She claims that many young people lack status, rights and power in society, arising:

> not only by dint of their perceived vulnerability because of age but also because they fall between the two stools of protection and dependence as children and autonomy and self-determination as adults. They are also often labelled by their elders as rebellious and troublesome, and phrases such as 'underclass youth' and 'dangerous youth' abound … they are set apart from mainstream society by the often limited understanding and increasing pessimism of adults, and many young people are doubly constrained by poverty, their extended dependence on the family and state in the transition to adulthood, and by limited opportunities available to them for higher education, employment, housing and citizenship. (Barry, 2005: 1)

In response, she points out that youth policy is 'one of the key vehicles for ensuring that young people's social inclusion becomes more of a reality' (Barry, 2005: 2). Challenging this alleged power imbalance and the often-negative discourse used to describe the current generation of young people clearly calls for the engagement of young people as creators, rather than merely receivers, or targets of policy.

Young people as 'active citizens'

The third typology of youth policy identifies young people as active citizens. However, the idea of young people participating in civic and public life is a broad church of interpretation and debate, and the concept of citizenship 'is one that continues to be problematic' (Lawson, 2001: 163). As already stated, the social investment in young people as the future of the nation now holds a central place in policy development. However, a core uncertainty surrounding the roles and responsibilities of young people as active citizens has also persisted. Many writers in the international field of youth studies have failed to agree on a common understanding of the role of young people as active citizens. What *has* been consistent is an acknowledgement of the period of 'youth' as representing a time of transition to the rights and responsibilities of adult citizenship (Jones and Wallace, 1992; Coles, 1995; Hall and Williamson, 1999; Storrie, 2004; Wood, 2009). The impact of policy mechanisms designed to control the movement of young people through the transitional stages to adulthood can result in a deferment of citizenship status, leading to a range of alternative descriptors including quasi-citizens, proto-citizens, apprentice citizens and citizens-in-waiting (Fyfe, 2003; Matthews, 2001; Hine and Wood 2009).

Therefore, the policy paradigms concerned more with successfully steering young people through the potential transitional mire to adulthood continue to dominate. The discourse that portrays young people as active citizens is built on their meaningful engagement with decision-making. Perkins advocates that:

> Young people have a right and a civic responsibility to participate and contribute to their communities. Active participation in the community is viewed as essential to the positive development of young people and ultimately to the success of communities and institutions. (Perkins, 2009: 108)

Without such community engagement, however, the potential risks associated with the transition process may result in young peoples' social exclusion, or a magnified focus on their perceived deviant behaviour. Ideally for today's young active citizen, accessing rights and responsibilities sits alongside tangible and accessible opportunities for practical forms of participation in civic and public life. Whilst the active citizen policy discourse clearly exhorts young people to act responsibly, success in this endeavour is contingent on the respective government or community fulfilling their responsibilities to enable the participation

(West, 1996). The community engagement agenda has shifted the old adage of young people being 'seen but not heard' to one where they are 'heard but not seen'. As Percy-Smith explains:

> The underlying problem for young people is not so much a lack of opportunities or a lack of voice, but rather not having the freedom to express themselves as equal citizens through their choices and actions as they use neighbourhood space. In spite of local consultation initiatives, young people's sense of marginalization in their neighbourhoods, both in terms of decision-making and everyday experiences, does not seem to change. (Percy-Smith, 2006: 158)

The emphasis within contemporary discourse on notions of community engagement and active participation has created a potential tension in the lives of young people in regard to citizenship. In one direction the public sphere is opening up the possibilities for involvement in decision-making at a younger age, whilst the impact of other policies results in an extension of the transitional pathways towards an independent life and the traditional markers of adulthood. As a result, access to the rights and responsibilities of citizenship for some young people may remain restricted. The chapter now moves to an analysis of the role and purpose of youth work in responding to the contemporary policy discourse affecting the lives of young people.

Youth work and community engagement

Youth work is concerned with the social, personal and political development of young people (Merton and Wylie, 2004). As discussed in Chapter 1, the origins of contemporary youth work practice lie in the mid-to-late nineteenth century. Historically, a core purpose of youth work was to achieve the 'salvation' of the participating children 'from the vices of their parent culture' (Blanch, 1979, quoted in Smith, 1988: 12). The portrayal of young people as the perceived enemy within their own communities appears to have been sustained over time. For example, the report *Measurement of Youth Crime in Scotland* concluded that:

> Public perceptions of and anxieties about crime have remained static (or worsened) during a period in which crime rates have been falling. Such findings have led to the identification of fear of crime as a focus for policy intervention in its own right and as a social condition that

is seen as virtually independent of crime and detection rates. Local authorities and police forces are thus increasingly tasked with reducing fear of crime through a 'reassurance' agenda. The activities of young people are a particular focus for such strategies, not surprisingly, since, by any measure, they contribute disproportionately to the crime rate and act as a focus for national and local concerns about crime and disorder. (Scottish Executive, 2005a: 10)

Ongoing research in this area confirms that general attitudes towards young people in Scotland appear largely unchanged and remain characterised by a tension between compassion for, and anxiety about, today's youth (Scottish Government, 2008d).

The dominant policy and practice response to this perceived ongoing tension has been influenced by a coercive hegemony that tends to react to the lifestyle choices made by young people. It is now commonplace for youth work practitioners to be engaged in projects concerned with managing and modifying the perceived risky and deviant behaviour of today's youth, rather than supporting them as active citizens in decision-making. This is clearly in sharp contrast to the goals of community engagement that are concerned with embracing the agency of young people in taking action on issues that concern them.

Moreover, service provision has become closely allied to available funding that mirrors political priorities; dictating a major shift in service provision. For example, the role played by youth work as a diversionary model of crime prevention, often disguised in the softer language of community safety (Jeffs, 1997). Youth work practitioners appear to be increasingly operating in a dialectical position between the policy demands of the state and the 'vices of the parent culture'. An apparent managerial culture of has taken hold in local communities, resulting in alternative forms of practice, both old and new running the risk of becoming marginalised. This is a situation foreseen over a decade ago by Tony Jeffs whereby:

> Traditions of practice which sought to foster participation and an engagement with democracy have increasingly been jettisoned ... the educational raison d'être which underpinned alternative methodologies has been sidelined as intervention has increasingly been justified on the basis of crime prevention or the management of the socially excluded. (Jeffs, 1998: 11)

Youth work practitioners have traditionally adopted informal learning, one of the principal methods of working with young people, as their *raison d'être* (Stanton, 2004). Such an approach encourages young people to make sense of their physical, moral, social and political worlds through a process of critical reflection, learning and action. For Jeffs and Smith (1990: 3) 'informal education is primarily an approach: a form of pedagogy'. The pedagogic agenda of youth work is dependent on the capacity of the practitioner to incorporate potential learning outcomes into activities in which young people are voluntarily engaged. And as such, learning in youth work is often experiential and reflexive; delivered through participation in activities, opportunities and experiences. Hall *et al.* (2000) argue that these components—voluntarism and experiential learning—distinguish youth work from the more formal education of young people. For Jeffs, there is an important and discernible difference:

> Youth workers can and do act as instructors feeding young people facts and information, as and when it is required they do so, but that is not the essence of their role. They do not merely pass-on the knowledge of others to young people. Good youth workers are active agents constantly seeking to identify and problematise the experiences of young people, to teach by reflecting back those experiences to young people for scrutiny. (Jeffs, 2004: 60)

The transmission of existing or tacit knowledge and skills engendered through diverse learning opportunities is an aspect of youth work practice particularly pertinent to contemporary debates about education for active citizenship. Across the UK and other comparable advanced democracies the task of preparing young people for the challenges of citizenship is consistently delegated to schools. However, youth work can, and should, enable young people to get to grips with the knowledge base that is an essential prerequisite for active citizenship.

Alongside this assertion of the potential role of youth work is the case to be made for youth participation in terms of the benefits it holds for young people themselves. Children and young people have the right to participate in decisions that affect their lives, the lives of their community and the larger society in which they live. This is a formal right enshrined in the United Nations Convention of the Rights of the Child (Article 12) (Scottish Government, 2008c). Youth participation should be embedded in decision-making at a local and national level where young people's involvement leads to more effective decision-making. Indeed, if young people are well engaged as partners in local decision-making they can be 'powerful change agents for the betterment of their community' (Perkins, 2009: 108–9).

A common accusation made at today's youth is that they are apathetic and disengaged from the structures and processes of democracy. This alleged malaise is described as a democratic or civic deficit; pejorative terms that appear persistently as a precursor to discussions around young people and political participation. A study on public attitudes to participation in Scotland (Scottish Executive, 2005b) confirmed that younger people were less likely to have been involved in campaign activities related to decision-making. Contrastingly, they were also less inclined to trust elected representatives to make decisions for them. The Report concluded:

> Young people appeared to be motivated by the same factors as everyone else and were also more positive about the role of devolution in making government more accessible. The issue for younger respondents appeared to be the extent to which they felt able to effectively contribute. (Scottish Executive, 2005b: 15)

It would seem then that young people have the desire and ability to act, if given the opportunity. Furthermore there is growing evidence to refute claims of young people's general disengagement from politics. They are participating in a range of ways on issues that matter to them 'not only the action structured through political institutions and non-government organisations but also involvement in less structured, looser networks and friendship circles' (Kovacheva, 2005: 27). Additionally, young people are more involved in individual action, such as consumer boycotts, and actions directed more towards community or cause-orientated social movements rather than the traditional structures and processes of representative democracy.

New technologies are also offering young people an alternative setting for community engagement. Through creative uses of electronic communication young people are accessing peer-led online platforms for information, critical discussion and exploring alternative forms of cultural expression. Young people are utilising social networking, internet blogging and online resources to support their active participation (Coleman and Rowe. 2005; Owen. 2006). As a result, new forms of participation have surfaced, which appear less institutionalised and more flexible that extend young people's engagement and our understanding of active citizenship. These new and different forms of active involvement in civic and public life ultimately enhance connections between young people and their communities. The chapter now focuses more closely on forms of youth participation and the challenges faced by practitioners in supporting young people's active engagement in civic and public life.

Approaches to youth participation

Approaches to youth participation can be conceptualised in four ways. First, through processes that test or gauge the opinion of young people on issues and services. This approach generates data that can inform decision-making. The second approach to youth participation is user involvement where young people have an active role in the management and governance of a particular agency, organisation or group. Many local community and neighbourhood centres have youth representatives on their management committees and boards. The scope of the decision-making power and influence in this role can vary. Third is civic participation that encompasses a broad range of formal structures and processes that operate often parallel to similar adult-oriented decision-making bodies. Examples of civic participation could include youth councils, forums, student councils and youth parliaments. In many cases the young people involved in these participative situations are elected representatives and advocates for their peers. Such organisations and groups can have a direct impact on policy and service provision through close working partnerships with local community projects, government departments and organisations. The fourth approach to youth participation is political activism. Young people are members of recognised political parties, groups, organisations, unions and social movements. Young people's engagement with politics can span the spectrum of conventional and non-conventional democratic participation. This includes actions such as electoral voting, campaigning, lobbying, petitioning, marches, demonstrations, creative protest and online activism. Much of this activity is directly related to influencing government policy and public services. Young people engage as political activists at different levels from local neighbourhoods to international global campaigns. Examples of these respective approaches are given in Table 5.2, overleaf.

Table 5.2   Approaches to Youth Participation

Testing Opinion   In Edinburgh the city-wide *Viewfinder* survey is conducted every three years to gather the opinions of young people on a range of topics including safety, work and money, the environment, leisure and transport. In 2007 over 18,000 young people participated in the study, the findings help shape the development and delivery of dedicated youth services in the city (www.youngedinburgh.org.). The biennial *Being Young in Scotland Survey* collects data from young Scots aged between 11 and 25. The recently published 2009 study involved over 2,000 young people; the findings provide up-to-date intelligence to inform policy and practice. (www.youthlinkscotland.org)

User Involvement   The Rock Trust is a charity that works in Edinburgh and West Lothian with homeless and socially excluded young people between the ages of 16 and 25. The organisation seeks to gain young peoples' involvement in all aspects of their work. The full involvement of young people helps build confidence that the services provided are both relevant and useful. All support services have young peoples' involvement groups attached to them that help to shape how each service is run. These groups also send representatives to the overall Young Persons Involvement Group—which has a direct link to the Board of Directors. (www.rocktrust.org)

Civic Participation   The Scottish Youth Parliament (SYP) was established in 1999 and comprises elected young people aged between 14 and 25 representing different geographical areas and voluntary organisations across Scotland. The Members (MSYPs) are elected every two years. The MSYPs periodically discuss and debate issues that affect young people and consult widely through organisations on topical issues of concern. MSYPs work directly with the Scottish Parliament through representation and evidence to committees and communication with politicians. The SYP provide Scotland's representation to the UK Youth Parliament. The SYP is an apolitical organisation in that MSYPs are not elected on the basis of affiliation to any political party or group. (www.syp.org.uk)

Political Activists   The Amnesty International UK Youth Urgent Action network is a team of activists aged 11–18 who take rapid action to protect individuals at risk and put an end to human rights violations wherever and whenever they occur. Amnesty support over 670 school groups in the UK who write letters, fundraise and organise events. As members of Amnesty young people are engaged in international alliances and campaign activities locally and globally to challenge injustice. (www.amnesty.org.uk)

These four discrete approaches do not stand alone. Young people may participate across the four and equally, organisations and groups may adopt different approaches in their work. Through categorising approaches to youth participation in this way core elements of each highlight the diverse range of knowledge and skills required by young people to engage effectively in the breadth of opportunities available to them. Also, the respective approaches result in different outcomes in terms of public influence and learning and development for the young people involved. Each of these approaches presents challenges and opportunities for youth work practitioners and other service providers. The next section shows how one organisation has worked in a holistic way with young people 'to support their community engagement.

West Lothian Youth Participation Network—engagement through collaboration

The West Lothian Youth Participation Network (WLYPN) was established in 2005 as a forum for practitioners interested and engaged in youth participation to come together to share information, knowledge and resources. The membership of the group includes representatives from a wide range of services located in the local authority, voluntary and charity sectors. The practitioners involved bring expertise in specific service provision, such as housing, health, children's rights, looked-after care and careers. In addition, particular groups of young people who are experiencing social exclusion on the grounds of sexual orientation, disability and homelessness are also represented by workers in those fields. The professional backgrounds of the group include youth workers, community education workers, social workers, community artists, health professionals, development workers and local authority service managers.

Through partnership working and a collective commitment to the promotion of young people's active participation, the diverse membership of WLYPN have developed a range of innovative approaches to practice. These have included hosting conferences on topics such as youth health and peer mediation, development of a forum focused on youth health issues, establishing a training and support network for peer mediation, development of a pupil council training programme, design and delivery of learning for democracy courses in local colleges and schools, launching the youth voter registration initiative, and supporting collaborative projects targeted at helping socially excluded groups of young people to explore critically social issues, and providing support to young people to influence decision-making at different levels.

One aspect of the activities supported by WLYPN captures the wide array of approaches to youth participation outlined above and brings to life some of challenges and potential outcomes of this work. The development of youth electoral participation has been a core aim of the network. Emphasis on this form of community engagement was borne out of research evidence that pointed to low levels of first-time voter registration and turnout in West Lothian when set alongside other comparable local authorities. The Democracy Challenge project was established with the specific aim of raising voter registration amongst young people. In collaboration with staff from the Electoral Registration Office, youth work practitioners embarked upon an informal educational programme that was structured around four elements; gauging how politics affects the lives of local young people, providing information about the electoral process, promotion of local opportunities for civic engagement and for those eligible, providing advice and support to complete the electoral registration form. The initiative involved over 2,000 young people aged 16–18 from 11 secondary schools and a further 150 young people not in mainstream schooling who were experiencing varied forms of social exclusion. There have been tangible outcomes from the Democracy Challenge project including increased knowledge and understanding of political issues and the electoral process, enhanced political efficacy, with the participating young people feeling more engaged in the political process and able to influence decision-making. The project has also generated baseline data to monitor the long-term impact of the work on future levels of voter registration.

Williamson (1997) suggests that youth work may be viewed as a 'playground' for the learning of citizenship. The work of WLYPN illustrates the value of practitioners collaborating with a shared commitment to developing an array of opportunities for community engagement that responds to the needs and interests of young people. A recurrent criticism of youth participation is that young people are asked for their views but never receive feedback or know if their views have produced any real change in policy or practice (Tisdall and Davis, 2004). In actual fact the demand for participation is such that:

> local or national governments or other organisations are aware they need to be *seen* to have consulted with children and young people … Being consulted does not mean that children and young people influence the result. (Tisdall *et al.*, 2008: 347)

Through adopting meaningful approaches to participation that position young people as key partners in decision-making there is less likelihood of such accusations. The real empowerment of young people requires a policy process and practice framework where the expressed agenda and actions of young people are recognised as relevant *and* taken seriously. Batsleer (2008: 146) stresses that their voices 'are easily discredited and ignored, even within systems that demand their participation'. It is therefore imperative that youth workers understand the decision-making structures and processes that affect young people's lives. The outcomes of the Democracy Challenge project had a clear impact on levels of community engagement by young first-time voters. The practitioners involved in WLYPN are working to ensure that youth participation is promoted through sharing good practice as well as celebrating achievements, successes and change arising from young people's engagement.

Conclusion—some challenges for youth work

Youth policy is designed in response to a range of conceptions of young people, and as a result has an ambition and responsibility for their reconstruction. Dominant public discourse and representations of today's youth are shaped by the tension between sympathy for and concern about the current generation of young people. The goals of community engagement open up opportunities to embrace and nurture their potential role as active citizens. Youth work offers a vehicle for the development of citizenship, in terms of achieving a critical knowledge base and putting the acquired skills into practice. Youth work practitioners should endeavour to tip the balance of power in favour of young people through methods and approaches that promote 'equality, mutuality, joint responsibility and empowerment' (Ord, 2007: 47). Youth participation is ultimately bound up in notions of power, without a deeper understanding of issues and the forces of power at play, participative practice runs the risk of becoming merely tokenistic consultation. The involvement of young people as active citizens provides opportunities for political expression and action (Helve, 1997). However, within the often-complex and contradictory relationship between young people and policy there remains an apparent need for a breadth of opportunities to become social and political actors. The collaborative work of the WLYPN provides an example of such an approach. Young people participate in doing things that are interesting, relevant and fun. The active engagement of young people in decision-making fosters their capacity and sense of connection, ownership and cohesion in the community (Perkins, 2009). Youth work can provide a creative and stimulating arena for young people to learn informally and exercise their role as citizens through community participation and engagement and ensure their 'great promise' is realised.

In the next chapter the possibilities for a more democratic society, in which people feel able to contribute and be listened to, are further explored. The focus will be on the role that community education can play in bringing about progressive social change.

Chapter 6

Community Education, Risk and the Education of Desire

> Increasingly we feel comfortable with seeing people as victims of their own circumstances rather than authors of their own lives. The outcome of these developments is a world that equates the good life with self-limitation and risk aversion. (Furedi, 1997: 147)

Introduction

A healthy democracy requires a robust civil society in which a variety of constituencies are capable of making their voices heard. Currently, however, whilst there is a great deal of rhetoric about the importance of empowering people to be more autonomous, powerful socio-economic pressures make this increasingly difficult. One of these pressures is a pervasive pessimism that issues such as 'globalisation' are beyond our control and it is impossible to protect others and ourselves from its effects. As the quotation at the start of the chapter reminds us, people are increasingly seen as victims of fate who cannot help themselves or work out their own responses to problems. In turn this creates an insidious dependence on experts to 'help' people deal with experiences 'appropriately' and this dependence can fuel mistrust of other sources of support such as friends, family and local communities. Belief in the power of fate, and doubts about people's ability to cope with life, undermine personal autonomy and responsibility whilst leading us to accept closer state regulation of behaviour (see Furedi, 1997: 150). This kind of 'therapeutic ethos' also erodes optimism that education and learning can enable people to change their lives and embeds an approach to people as 'psychologically deficient' (Ecclestone, 2004: 131) and therefore unable to take decisions for themselves. Indeed, as Usher and Edwards (1998: 217) point out, 'the most effective forms of power are those which are not recognised as powerful because they are cloaked in the esoteric "objective" knowledge of expertise and the humanistic discourse of helping and empowerment'.

Another aspect of this discourse is that it makes changing from what is seen as 'normal' behaviour in a community or family seem to be risky. So if participating in education and learning is viewed as not for people like you then you are unlikely to want to go against dominant norms. This is compounded by the issue that the essence of risk is about what *might be* happening rather than what *is* happening because anticipating what is risky only suggests what should *not* be done, not what *should* be done (Adam *et al.*, 2000). This means that risks are about anticipating something that has not yet happened. What it is possible to anticipate, however, is based on a set of gendered, 'raced' and classed assumptions that are taken for granted and unconscious and so they structure experiences that are hidden from view.

It seems important to challenge these discourses that constrain the capability of people to take control of their own lives otherwise compliance, rather than change, will be the result. This chapter seeks to examine whether community education can make a difference to people's lives through challenging these 'victim' discourses. It will consider strategies that can encourage people to take back control. One important consideration is how the ability of all citizens can be acknowledged so that people can define their own problems and find appropriate solutions. Policy documents (SOEID, 1999, Communities Scotland and Scottish Executive, 2004; COSLA and Scottish Government, 2008) have identified working in partnership, building community capacity and promoting active citizenship as important ways in which community educators can help marginalised communities to become more socially included. The language of policy documents may be more rhetorical than real, but such rhetoric does provide opportunities for community educators to apply these policy initiatives in ways that contribute towards building a more equal society. This chapter will begin by providing examples that have focused on these issues and then move on to see if there are more radical ways in which to bring about progressive social change.

Working in partnership to build community capacity

Traditionally, services have been delivered to the public with limited consultation and involvement. One way of strengthening local democracy is to make it more responsive to the changing needs of communities and to strive to involve people in the processes of economic and social regeneration. Scottish policy states that building community capacity should involve 'a focus on community regeneration' (Scottish Executive, 2002: 11) and for community educators this involves working with communities to help them play a significant role in shaping the type of services available to them and in determining how they should be delivered. Working with a range of partners from both the public and the private sectors has been identified by the Scottish Government (e.g. 2008b) as one way in which local people can become involved in the regeneration of their communities.

This important area of work clearly requires the active involvement of community representatives in implementing appropriate action if it is to succeed. However, there are a number of difficulties that arise out of the social and geographical segregation of communities and these are downplayed in government policies, where there is an assumption that communities are homogenous and so achieving consensus among the community participants is seen as relatively unproblematic. For example, the Scottish Executive (2000d) suggested that 'services need to listen to their communities with a single ear. Having listened they need to change the services they provide and the way in which they are delivered in a way that is more responsive to their communities' needs.' In contrast, research shows the conflictual character of co-ordinating different and unequal interest and identity groups, and therefore the crucial question of differential power relations (Hatcher and Leblond, 2001). This means it is important to distinguish between involvement in decision-making and empowerment to take decisions and also between strategic power and operational power. Some partners may have the strategic power to set the agendas whilst others only have the operational power to participate in the implementation of agendas set by others. In other words, partnerships for regeneration are characterised by processes of inclusion and exclusion. Just as some potential partners may be wholly or partially excluded, so others may be compulsorily included: projects that are presented as 'partnerships' are not entirely the product of voluntary collaboration. In the case of the Social Inclusion Partnerships, for example, community representatives and activists were often designated as 'partners' and incorporated into the planning process whether they desired it or not (see Tett, 2005).

Another problematic area results from the differences between partners in terms of their influence. Community representatives are more likely to have limited access to information compared with private and public sector partners and so are less able to make appropriate interventions. This issue is exacerbated by the way in which partnerships for regeneration are implemented. Additional resources are only available for a limited time, have to be spent quickly, and so few opportunities are provided for careful consultation and consolidation. Such partnership initiatives rarely provide long-term sustainable funding and often fold, with the resulting demoralisation of the community that is left to cope with the fallout. This also highlights the importance of giving sufficient recognition to the resources that are provided on a continuing basis within communities rather than simply concentrating on new resources that are provided for new initiatives. Communities consistently provide the human resources of voluntary effort and enthusiasm that sustain informal patterns of community care and community solidarity but these are often ignored (Mayo, 1997: 11).

Area-based initiatives in themselves can exacerbate fragmentation and ine-quality of provision across communities because some areas become more successful at gaining funds that are bid for on a competitive basis. Moreover, disadvantaged communities are further pathologised where remedies concerned with social exclusion are directed at the community and family rather than the underpinning socio-economic structures. As Nancy Fraser points out:

> Although the approach aims to redress economic injustice, it leaves intact the deep structures that generate class disadvantage. Thus, it must make surface reallocations again and again. The result is to mark the most disadvantaged class as inherently deficient and insatiable, as always needing more and more. (Fraser, 1997: 25)

The demands of partnership, the lack of time and resources to build the cap-acity of community participants and the need to show results quickly make it difficult to spread commitment throughout communities (Purdue *et al.*, 2002). This means that the work of community representation is concentrated on too few community groups who may not have either the time or commitment to consult other community members properly. In regeneration partnerships funders often predetermine those that are able to represent 'the community' and this intensifies the difficulties of representing the disparate interests that exist in any community (Russell, 2001). This is a particular problem for black and minority ethnic communities, which are often treated as if their interests are homogenous and are rarely resourced in a way that can give voice to their many different members (Craig et al, 2002).

Given these difficulties with community capacity-building how might com-munities and the community educators who work with them be more effectively empowered through participating in partnerships for socio-economic renewal? Partnerships for regeneration are potentially creative but they can founder unless they are based on shared interests, and are operating with agreed mechanisms for negotiating differences. One key is that they must be set in the context of longer-term strategies for community development that offer possibilities for renewal. If communities are to be fully involved then maximum access to as much inform-ation as possible is needed, particularly research that will enable them to justify alternative views. Participatory action research is one way in which communities can build more systematic knowledge bases from their own experiences as a counter-weight to external, specialist knowledge. In addition, structures need to be in place so that they can influence decision-making through developing their own ideas and agendas, proactively. They also need to have access to independ-ent specialist advice that would enable them to develop their own policy analysis. Having control over resources of money, time and staff is also a powerful tool in establishing a more equal place at the partnership table. If these conditions were met then communities would be better placed to:

> play an active role in setting the agenda and pressing for the wider policy changes required. [This kind of partnership for renewal would then be able to meet] social needs as defined from the bottom up, rather than responding to the requirements of market-led agendas determined from the top down. (Mayo, 1997: 24)

Community educators have an important role to play in assisting commu-nities to understand, operate within, and challenge their political environment. This involves identifying and stressing areas of commonality and the creative development of links and alliances between groups that might otherwise see themselves as being in competition. It also involves recognising the rights of those who experience problems to define appropriate solutions and campaign for their implementation, often against the vested interests of the powerful. These are the spaces that communities create for themselves that are less marked by the considerable differences in status and power that exist in formal partner-ships. These can be contrasted to what Andrea Cornwall (2005) has named 'invited spaces' where opportunities to participate are structured and owned by those that provide them. In these spaces it is difficult for community repre-sentatives to be active and equal partners in decision-making especially when they disagree with the proposals of the other, more powerful members of the partnership. In such circumstances the resulting conflict and disagreement often leads the other partners to silence the community's dissenting voices by marginalising their perspective. Becoming incorporated into a partnership that seeks to achieve goals that are not in the community's interest can silence criticism. The result is a forced consensus: one that assumes the community will comply but actually masks profound disagreement. It is at this point that decisions have to be made about whether the best interests of the community would be served by remaining within a partnership or campaigning from the outside. Campaigning with the community for their issues to be represented, however, is likely to be a more productive option if community voices are marginalised.

In these circumstances community educators have an important role to play in educating the more powerful partners so that they see this kind of community capacity-building as an opportunity for impoverished communities to take action based on their own interests, rather than as a potential threat to their professional positions. Capacity building is about supporting people in expressing their own ideas rather than categorising them as the 'socially excluded' or 'troublesome youth' and enables people to see themselves not as objects of social intervention but as subjects who may want to operate in opposition to these negative, deficit, identities. It also means that spaces for participation in decision-making have to be located in the places in which they occur so that the possibilities are framed with reference to their actual political, social and historical particularities (see Cornwall, 2008).

Developing active citizenship

Extending public involvement in the democratic process has been an important goal of governments. Community education, through its role in engaging with people in communities around their interests, has been identified as having a key role to play in developing active citizenship. Citizenship is a difficult concept to define, as was discussed in the previous chapter, although there are broadly two main types of understanding. One conception sees it as a status bestowed on those people who are full members of a community with the rights and obligations that flow from that membership. Another conception attaches importance to the social relationships that enable people to actively participate in decision-making in their social, economic, cultural and political life (Lister, 1997: 29). The first conception gives priority to status and the second to citizenship as an active practice. This latter conception prioritises the ability of people who are disadvantaged, in terms of power and resources, to exercise their civil and political rights effectively in order to achieve their valued goals. This involves promoting their free and equal participation, in both defining the problems to be addressed and the solutions to be used, in ways that mitigate economic and social inequalities. It requires a public space in which different groups can come together to air their differences and build solidarity around common interests.

By prioritising citizenship as active participation in the governance of the community, community educators could help to counter and replace the more common assumption that people have the status of either clients or consumers. The active participation of ordinary people in creating the projects that shape their selves, as well as the communities in which they live, provides a reason for working together with others to secure trusting relations within the community. Communities that learn to create institutional arrangements that include a whole variety of voices in their deliberations are likely to be more democratically just and thus robust and capable enough to address the difficult problems that they face in the twenty-first century. The possibility of shared understanding requires not only the valuing of others but also the creation of communities in which mutuality and consequently the conditions for learning can flourish. As Stewart Ranson suggests:

> There is no solitary learning: we can only create our worlds together. The unfolding agency of the self grows out of the interaction with others. It is inescapably a social creation. (Ranson, 1998: 20)

Citizenship politics can be oppositional and disruptive when community groups prioritise issues that might become challenges to dominant interests and agendas. For example, non-violent direct action against the closing down of a local school prioritises a different vision of what might be for the good of the community from that proposed by the local authority. These kinds of struggles provide a local arena for people to exercise their citizenship in ways that they often find more engaging than broader national issues. As a process this can both strengthen excluded communities and, through collective action, promote the citizenship of individuals within those communities. As Ruth Lister points out:

> Such action can boost individual and collective self-confidence, as individuals and groups come to see themselves as political actors and effective citizens. This is especially true for women for whom involvement in community organisations can be more personally fruitful

than engagement in formal politics that are often experienced as more alienating than empowering. (Lister, 1997:33)

Placing value on informal politics does not, however, mean ignoring the continuing need both to open up formal political areas and to make formal politics more accountable to the informal.

People have the fundamental right as citizens to be listened to within the process of decision-making. Members of communities need to recognise each other as citizens who share a common status and equal rights but this is difficult given that we live increasingly within communities of difference. Ours is a heterogeneous society with many different voices, which means that people can be excluded from participation in democratic decision-making in two broad ways. One way is by failing to recognise people's cultural differences and the other is through the inequality of distribution of socio-economic resources. The challenge for a strengthened local democracy is to discover processes that can reconcile the valuing of difference with the need for shared understanding and agreement about public purpose that dissolves prejudice and discrimination. People's interests therefore need to be represented in public debates both in terms of their cultural conditions and their material class interests. An inclusive citizenship requires the recognition of different voices as well as the fair distribution of resources that provide the conditions for equal participation. The challenge is to establish an understanding that embraces both the recognition of people's voices and the redistribution of resources in order to create a just, inclusive democracy.

There is a danger, however, that what is said to be an appropriate response to different cultures and religions actually rationalises oppressive practices because it makes inappropriate assumptions about minority ethnic cultures. Failure to challenge such hidden racism legitimates discrimination against particular sections of society and consequently other vulnerable groups. One example of citizenship education that addresses the recognition of different voices is anti-racist work. This involves confronting the reality of racism and developing a comprehensive and proactive strategy of anti-racist policy and practice. For community educators this requires making racism visible and recognising it as a daily reality for black and minority ethnic communities. One aspect of this action involves these communities, who are largely marginalised when it comes to having their voices heard, leading the process of shaping future action against racism. It also

must require members of the white majority community to address their responsibility as citizens to understand racism and counteract it and also to incorporate into policy and practice the voices of those suffering the effects of racism.
Making the connections between racism and other forms of inequality is crucial
if communities are to see the common problems that unite them. As Rowena
Arshad (1999: 288) points out, 'anti-racist education must speak the language of
rights (not needs), of life-chances (not lifestyles), of dismantling structures (not
merely reforming them)'. It also involves organising not *for* culture, but *against*
racism and the erosion of civil liberties, and *against* injustice and *for* equality,
as common causes. Such action for racial justice must begin from 'the experience and the aspirations of those who have been on the receiving end of racism'
(Arshad, 1999: 288). When black and white people work together in anti-racist
alliances a politics of solidarity can be created.

Communities need to be open to mutual recognition of the different perspectives and alternative views of the world in ways that allow pre-judgements
to be challenged so that assumptions can be amended and an enriched understanding of others can be developed. The key to the transformation of prejudice
lies in developing an understanding that leads people beyond their initial positions to take account of others and develop a richer, more comprehensive view.
Discussion lies at the heart of learning because through dialogue people learn to
take a wider, more differentiated view and thus acquire sensitivity, subtlety and
capacity for judgement. Identities are respected and compromises, if not consensus, are reached between rival traditions. By providing forums for participation
and voice, conditions for mutual accountability can be created so that citizens
can take each other's needs and claims into account in order to create the conditions for each other's development. As Ralph Miliband suggests:

> Education for citizenship means above all the nurturing of a capacity
> and willingness to question, to probe, to ask awkward questions, to
> see through obfuscation and lies. [It requires] the cultivation of an
> awareness that the request for individual fulfilment needs to be com-
> bined with the larger demands of solidarity and concern for the public
> good. (Miliband, 1994: 96)

Educating desire

So far this chapter has considered engagement with communities that has
focused on combating disadvantage and making changes within the existing

structures that would lead to improvements in people's lives. This section examines how far those with a more radical vision of community education could work with 'social movements' in order to provide progressive social change. Members of social movements subscribe to a common cause that is expressed collectively and embody a set of beliefs that reflect their shared values and purposes. Social movements, such as the women's movement, or the disability rights campaign or the coalition against poverty, all act to critique the existing social order, highlighting inadequacies and offering new ways of thinking. For example, the women's movement emphasised that apparently personal issues, such as the time spent on caring for the family, were actually political issues that required public action to ensure that public provision was available for childcare. Another example is the mental health survivors' movement that has challenged the hegemony of psychiatrists to determine what is wrong with them and instead emphasised the value of seeing the world differently (Crossley, 2004).

Social movements contribute to social change through politicising areas of experience that were previously excluded from the political agenda. For example, the Lesbian, Gay Bisexual and Transgender (LGBT) movement has challenged dominant constructions of sexuality, masculinity and femininity, and shown how they are socially constructed by dominant cultural norms. Social movements also 'generate dissidence and dissent from the dominant social and cultural values that inform our common sense and daily life' (Crowther, 2006: 180). Environmental action groups, for example, engaging in action against building a motorway have made the links between the global and local environment in pursuing a greener democracy. This has been an effective way to challenge the climate of opinion where media images of activists, potentially putting their lives at risk for a wider cause, has forced discussion of these issues on to the political agenda.

People who participate in social movements engage in significant collective learning that contributes to the creation of a critically informed public through the dissemination of ideas, values and beliefs that are in opposition to the status quo. Creating spaces in which possibilities can be explored, boundaries pushed and alternative action explored means that people become actors in the political process rather than passive observers of others' activity. The important task for community educators is to find ways of working with social movements that extend what is learned whilst, at the same time, achieving successful social action. This type of relationship suggests a very different educational process from the traditional one where the educator defines what it is relevant to learn.

Instead educators become resources for social movements and the respective curriculum built around the interests of their members.

The educative potential of social movements is not limited to those directly participating in them. As well as the challenges that they provide to 'common sense' and dominant ways of thinking, many movements seek to influence the public agenda by posing counter-positions and so challenging the limitations of the taken for granted. One example is the Rape Crisis (2009) campaign *This is not an invitation to rape me* that used a series of graphic media images to highlight the problem of institutionalised and culturally endorsed male violence against women and the resulting myths about the causes of rape. Campaigning against sexual violence highlights the importance of seeing the political as encompassing personal, domestic and social relations rather than only being about voting and democratic representation.

The autonomy of groups to define their own problems and develop their own organisational structures leads to a more genuinely democratic structure. Building alliances as a way of realising their vision is a key task for social movements that is clearly political but it is educational too. The educational opportunities presented by working with such groups that are committed to progressive social change can be enormous. Working to develop a curriculum from the social context of individual experience requires identifying any underlying contradictions. For example, the experience of being disabled includes dependency, and the analysis of what this means should be regarded as an educational resource rather than a problem to be solved. The idea of activists as learners also connects with the historical tradition of radical social action that emerged out of industrialisation and the consequential changes in social structures in which political analysis was regarded as a prerequisite for transformative social change. Educational engagement with dissenting citizens poses quite starkly the choice of developing an enriched democratic curriculum against incorporation into passive participation. As Paulo Freire pointed out:

> There is no such thing as a neutral education process. Education either functions as an instrument that is used to facilitate the integration of the young into the logic of the present system and bring about conformity to it or it becomes the practice of freedom. [Education then becomes] the means by which men and women deal critically and creatively with reality and discover how to participate in the transformation of the world. (Freire, 1972: 56)

This means that expressing the social nature of our experience and support-ing social movements that act to transform the world are legitimate educational aims. This also involves raising people's consciousness so that they become more aware of how their personal experiences are connected to larger societal prob-lems and historical and global processes.

Social movements have also played an important part in stretching our imag-ination about alternative ways of being because they open up questions about what we value and how we want to live. They ask questions about what type of society we want for the future and thus 'inject critique, vision and imagination into what we have learnt to take for granted' (Crowther, 1999: 36). By seeing the world as it is and how it might be, social movements are intrinsically utopian. In this sense utopia's proper role is to stir the imagination and challenge com-fortable habits—a place to be desired rather than a place that does not exist — leading to a vision of a much better world. Community education too should be concerned with the world as it could be, as much as with the world as it is. It is important to begin questioning our desires and to test them against other desires in order to explore what is possible for the future. As E. P. Thompson (1976: 790) commented, utopia's proper space is the education of desire in order 'to open a way to aspiration, to desire better, to desire more, and above all to desire in a different way'.

One example of the 'education of desire' is the disability movement, which aims to bring about structural and cultural changes to ensure that disabled people can have the same possibilities, and be supported by the same rights, as their non-disabled contemporaries. It has challenged the discourse of personal handicap and shown instead how society erects disabling attitudinal, organisa-tional and environmental barriers that exclude many of its citizens. Rather than looking at individual lifestyles it poses a more holistic and collective approach to change. The movement changed the focus of activity in relation to disability away from organisations *for* disabled people to organisations controlled and run *by* disabled people. They stress autonomy and the importance of self-organisa-tion as a challenge to the myth of passivity and the objectification of disabled people that results from underlying oppressive ideologies and social relations. As Tom Shakespeare (1993: 263) points out, 'in making "personal troubles" into "public issues", disabled people are affirming the validity and importance of their own identity, rejecting the victimising tendencies of society at large, and their own socialisation'.

An aspect of this change of consciousness has been for disabled people to adopt a 'disabled identity' with the same vigour and sense of purpose as has been achieved in other social movements such as the LBGT movement. 'This necessarily involves the subordination of individual circumstances to a shared sense of identity and experience of social oppression, and a united opposition to a disabling society' (Barnes *et al.*, 1999: 174). The process of positive identification for disabled people is made difficult by the existence of internalised oppression, coupled with segregation and isolation from sources of collective support and strength. Nevertheless, the movement has been an educational force for change both within disability organisations and through its campaigning role in educating the wider world. It has enabled disabled people to desire a better life and thus to campaign actively for their human, civil and political rights through consciousness-raising and education.

Conclusion

Community educators have a number of ways of encouraging individuals and groups to be involved in making things happen rather than being told what to do by 'experts' or have things happen to them. It is vital that this be achieved through dialogue rather than through pre-established and arbitrary forms of power. The policy areas of working in partnership, building community capacity and promoting active citizenship provide real opportunities for community educators to make a positive difference in marginalised people's lives through their engagement in learning. Educators have an important role in making sure that the complexity of the intellectual, emotional, practical, pleasurable and political possibilities of learning is not reduced to the apparent simplicity of targets, standards and skills (see Thompson, 2000). Finding a voice to do this can happen through being part of a social, mutually supportive group that is engaged in learning. Such learning is a political, as well as an educational, activity because spaces are opened up for the public discussion of the issues with which people are concerned. Active groups can force into the public domain aspects of social conduct such as violence against women in the home and means that their voices 'help to contest the traditional, the official, the patriarchal and the privileged view of things' (Thompson, 2000: 143).

An emphasis on whose experiences count, and how they are interpreted and understood, helps us to challenge the 'common sense' of everyday assumptions about experience and its relationship to knowledge production. This allows new claims to be made for the legitimacy of reflexive experience leading to 'really useful knowledge' for those who are involved in generating it. In questioning the discourses that frame the ways of thinking, problems, and practices that are regarded as legitimate, it begins to be possible for people to open up new ways of reflexively thinking about the social construction of their experiences. When people create their own knowledge and have their voices heard, narrow definitions of what is thought to be 'educated knowledge' and who it is that makes it, are thrown into question. In this way the experiences and stories that have been excluded, and the mystification caused by 'expert' knowledge, can be interrogated as a way of articulating views that come from below rather than above. This is important 'because, in identifying and making spaces where alternative ways of thinking and being can be worked up, such practices increase the possibilities of knowledge—that is knowledge that is useful to those who generate it' (Barr, 1999: 82).

The final chapter will consider what possibilities for democracy and equality are offered for community educators to make a positive difference in collaboration with subordinated and marginalised people.

Chapter 7

Community Education, Democracy and Equality

Although natural endowments differ profoundly, it is the mark of a civilized
society to aim at eliminating such inequalities as having their source not in
individual differences, but in its own organisation. (Tawney, 1926: 27)

Introduction

This book has engaged with the debate surrounding the role, purpose, focus and
methodology of community education. It has shown how community education
can respond to people's own concerns by creating shared spaces where a variety
of perspectives can be discussed and commonalities developed. The changes in
community education that come about through what is emphasised, and what is
omitted, in policy and practice have been discussed and the book has provided a
wide range of illustrations from different contexts. It has also shown how these
presences and absences in policy and practice work to shape particular social
ends through examples from Europe, the UK and Scotland. Arising from this
analysis the emphasis has been on action that encourages people to express their
communality rather than simply their self-interest.

The ambiguous and shifting territory within which community education
operates is characterised by different understandings of how engaging in learning
can improve people's social and economic conditions. On the one hand, there is
an emphasis on the improvement of people's skills, achievements and individual
capabilities through learning whilst, on the other, there is a wider focus on the
economic and social forces that exclude people and how these forces might be
overcome. This debate is clearly visible in Scottish policies where the focus lies
mainly in enabling individuals to become 'better educated, more skilled and
more successful' (COSLA and Scottish Government 2008: 5). This emphasis
on the importance of individual differences is not new but has been present in

policy discourses about the underlying causes of inequalities for a long time, as the opening quotation illustrates.

For community educators, too, there are tensions that arise from their concerns to respond to the educational needs of social movements and communities generated from below, and their need to respond to state policies generated from above. Moreover, the approach of community educators that looks to the lived experience of people in communities to build the educational curriculum can simply reinforce the lowest common denominator, rather than challenging and stretching people. Such a situation demands that workers are self-critical about the implementation of their practice. Moreover, education that is rooted in the interests and experience of ordinary people can and should contribute to a more inclusive society, especially when it is seen from the standpoint of those who have the least power. So, what are the possibilities provided by the educational traditions of Scotland that would contribute to this difficult educational task of promoting democracy and equality?

Democratic renewal and the Scottish generalist tradition

There are a number of educational traditions in Scotland that make an important contribution to our understandings of greater democracy. Scotland provides an interesting exemplar for the study of democratic renewal because, as Ian Martin (1999: 2) has argued, it is both a mirror that reflects processes such as globalisation now at work in most societies, and a lens through which to examine these processes. He goes on to say that as a mirror Scotland reflects the current shifting of the boundaries between the state, the market and civil society that 'demands greater democracy and autonomy in order to facilitate a new kind of settlement between the cultural formation of the nation and the political formation of the state. As a lens Scotland provides an opportunity to see the beginnings of what could be a new kind of democracy at work 'by developing a more pluralistic and participative political culture'.

There are some grounds for claiming that there is a greater commitment to participation and equality in Scotland, at least in relation to the widening of opportunities. Participation in formal politics is becoming more widespread due to a number of mechanisms developed by the Scottish Parliament since its inception in 1999. One such mechanism is the ability to raise a petition to make a request for the Parliament to take a view on a matter of public interest or concern, or amend existing legislation or introduce new legislation. Another mechanism is the seeking of evidence by Parliamentary Committees from a wide range of groups, especially from the voluntary sector, a refreshing addition to the 'usual suspects' seen as the authority on particular issues. Recently this has included the Anti-Poverty Alliance, whose members have been able to show the detrimental effects of living in poverty and enabled Parliament to listen to evidence from those with insider expertise of the experience of poverty in their day-to-day lives. A third example is the Scottish Youth Parliament that comprises nearly 200 elected young people aged between 14 and 25, who aim to be the collective national youth voice for all young people in Scotland. The Scottish Youth Parliament meets three times a year to discuss issues that affect young people and tries to propose innovative solutions to these problems and situations. A range of youth forums and councils throughout Scotland supported by community educators feed information and ideas into the Youth Parliament, and these bodies were instrumental in pushing for its establishment. Of course these mechanisms do not necessarily lead to the real delegation of responsibility, nor prepare people for taking decisions democratically, nor necessarily lead to greater equality, but they are important steps on the way to a more democratic society.

Some of these changes in the workings of democracy have been fuelled by a cultural tradition most cogently explored by George Davie in his book *The Democratic Intellect: Scotland and Her Universities in the Nineteenth Century* (1961). Davie pointed out the need for interdisciplinarity in educational practice and consequently the value of the generalist rather than the specialist, and drew attention to the civic and educational power generated when one area of thought or expertise is illuminated by another. This generalist approach values the expert as part of the community but recognises that his or her value can only be realised if it is accepted that blind spots within the expert view are inevitable. Thus others within the community by virtue of their lack of expertise (which gives them a different perspective from that of the expert) have a responsibility to comment on these blind spots. The problems that this approach sought to address were those of over-specialisation and a narrow focus on the technicalities of how to get things done. The case for the generalist tradition was the need to get to the root issues and causes of problems, in democratically informed ways, before questions of detail were addressed.

This historical tradition provides the basis for a distinctive vision of a rich and humane civic culture that remains relevant and worth working for today. Davie's argument for a democratic intellect in higher education, where non-specialists were encouraged to interrogate specialists, is a vital part of a healthy society and can equally be applied to community education. The belief that an educated community of specialists are unfit to make decisions without processes of scrutiny leads to an understanding that they are, in effect, intellects without democracy. The issue for the community educator is how to develop a curriculum that can facilitate the mutual illumination of blind spots in the sense referred to above. What is essential is to engage the critical intellect of people in a way that creates more rounded human beings and enables people to engage with public issues. Community education is about the development of knowledge and skills, building human relationships and the engagement of people in understanding the wider social forces that impact both locally and globally. If people are to gain a voice they will need the confidence and authority that comes out of experience tempered by study, which provides opportunities for people to read the meaning between the lines and the interests behind the meaning (see Crowther and Tett, 2001). For example, tackling racism requires the expertise of those who have directly suffered its effects as well as the general knowledge of those who seek to understand and counteract it. Understanding disability includes an awareness of the meaning of dependency, which becomes an educational resource both for disabled experts and interested generalists, rather than simply a technical problem to be solved. To live full lives people need an education that can equip them to develop their autonomy and control both at the individual and the communal level. As the Scottish Executive (2000d: 12) has argued in relation to young people, 'Scotland needs the contribution of all our young people, stemming the waste of underachievement, isolation and exclusion which blights many young lives.'

Redistribution and recognition

How might this democratic tradition be used to promote greater equality through addressing the learning needs of excluded groups and communities? There are always political choices to be made about the aims of development, and the state is not always clear about how its policies in these areas are to be implemented. These ambiguities lead to political and ethical choices for community educators if they wish to create a more equitable society that has the values of freedom, equality and solidarity at its heart. A commitment to meeting people's needs for a basic income, employment, health care, housing and education also requires the mutual recognition of worth, dignity and respect. Such a society would involve both the redistribution of goods and services to those who currently lack them and the recognition of the differentiated cultural, emotional and social knowledge that people have. The association of learning with economic skills would be broken and equal emphasis would be given to qualities allied more with care giving: sensitivity, patience, empathy and compassion. In other words, habits of mind that are often relegated to what Wendy Luttrell (1997) calls 'the ontological basement of different ways of knowing'. When knowledge is conceived as split between intellect and emotion, affect and cognition, autonomy and relatedness the knowledge that people feel able to claim for themselves is fragmented.

Operating within a democratic tradition would require community educators to stimulate and support learning and development to reduce inequalities through:

- exploring the contradictions of policy in ways that challenge discrimination and oppression;
- developing a curriculum that builds on what people already know and can do but also challenges them to take risks and develop further;
- acknowledging the value and importance of care and love as a contribution to knowledge and understanding;
- helping people to recognise that they have the capacity to learn and to generate new, 'really useful' knowledge;
- working on both increasing skills and developing people's critical awareness of why they might not have these skills in the first place;
- using learning to build community capacity and increase individual and collective self-confidence.

Education can contribute to the extension of social democracy but this requires the valuing of difference as well as the need for shared understanding and agreement. The experiences of marginalised groups and communities and their own definition of their needs are central to the organisation and delivery of appropriate education and other services. People themselves can develop their own forms of knowledge and this challenges the power of expert knowledge to monopolise the definition of what is wrong in their communities and what is needed to make it right. It requires a democratising of the relationship between users and providers, both collectively and individually, and a sharing of expert and lay knowledges. As Fiona Williams argues:

> Solidarities need to be developed that are based on respect for difference: not the solidarity of the lowest common denominator, nor the solidarity that assumes that all will forgo their particularities in a common goal, rather it is the pursuit of unity in dialogues of difference. Such politics also has to involve both the redistribution of goods and the mutual recognition of worth. (Williams, 1999: 684)

This is a very demanding task for community educators to help to achieve. However, if groups simply pursue the politics of recognition without addressing socio-economic inequalities, then they might win social justice for some in their group, but not for others. On the other hand, the singular pursuit of issues of economic inequality can make invisible cultural injustices that render some groups, such as minority ethnic communities or marginalised young people, more vulnerable to economic exploitation.

It is at the level of communities that people often get their first experience of democracy. Therefore, expanding opportunities for democratic life should start here where, for many people, they can engage directly in issues that affect their everyday lives. In the current context, however, a good deal of interest in participation may work against democratic life, rather than for it. For example, when community activists become incorporated into an externally created partnership that seeks to achieve goals that are not in the community's interest, criticism can be silenced. There are also problems with tokenism, in which, for example, the one black person on a committee is burdened with the expectation of being able to 'speak for' the entire community from which he or she comes. The development of local coalitions against exclusion, however, can lead to the development of a political culture that emphasises the fundamentally unequal nature of society rather than people's individual deficits. Emphasising the importance of redistributing resources also shows that there are alternatives to increasing inequalities that do not entirely rely on individual action. In this sense the democratic approach is about more than having a voice in services, however important that is. 'It is also about how we are treated and regarded more generally, and with having a greater say and control over the whole of our lives' (Beresford and Croft, 1993: 9). Popular participation in these more active forms of local politics therefore needs to become central to the processes of democracy. This will involve community educators in providing support to help people to influence policy through *advocating* community priorities rather than *negotiating* change based on the parameters set by policy directives.

Conclusion

Community education as a profession is always in a state of flux, as was noted in Chapter 2, and undoubtedly more changes are on their way. The work of community educators, whether their focus is on young people, adults or community capacity building, will always concentrate on purposeful learning and education in communities designed to bring about change. This book has attempted to show that community education can make an important contribution towards the building of a more democratic, equal, society. However, there are powerful ideological and economic forces that seek to dominate, oppress and exploit people and 'the democratic state must learn how to foster the civic autonomy of communities—rather than seek, as too often in the past, to co-opt and incorporate them' (Martin, 1999: 19). Government policies provide both problems and possibilities for community educators to help to develop a clearer analysis of the nature of inequality and oppression. In order to do this, the knowledge and experiences of those that have been excluded need to be valued and the mystification caused by 'expert' knowledge requires to be interrogated. Having a greater say in services is important, but being treated as capable citizens, with a right to dissent from provided solutions, is much more empowering and can lead to democratic renewal for all people. A popular curriculum that addresses the concerns of ordinary people and actively draws upon their experience as a resource for educational work in communities increases the possibilities of developing knowledge that is useful to those who generate it. People then act both as experts regarding their own lives and as generalists too, commenting on others' blind spots about the root issues and the causes of problems in communities.

Approaching education and democracy in this way would not be new but would involve revisiting much earlier debates over the role of education, as Margaret Davies argued in 1913:

> Even a little knowledge is a dangerous thing. It causes a smouldering discontent, which may flame into active rebellion against a low level of life, and produces a demand, however stammering, for more interests and chances. Where we see ferment, there has been some of the yeast of education. (Quoted in Scott, 1998: 56)

If community educators wish to see a fairer society then 'the yeast of education' will need to be applied to its work with communities through ensuring that people's concerns and realities are put at the centre. This means focusing on issues such as violence and discrimination against people who are seen as 'different', improving people's economic, physical and mental health needs and organising learning in ways that do not further isolate people from each other. This approach will be based on the notion of community education as a *'dissenting vocation'* that takes the side of ordinary people against the ideological and economic forces that seek to dominate, oppress and exploit them (see Martin, 2001). For people to be perceived by others, and to see themselves, as visible and valuable and to learn to speak with their authentic voices they need to be able to create their own knowledge. Members of communities would then be perceived as active citizens making demands for change with their different ways of knowing and understanding the world being valued as a resource for learning.

Rather than seeking to minimise risk, community educators should be 'educating desire' through challenging and supporting marginalised people to define and solve their problems for themselves. Doing this is risky because it requires courage and spirited conviction for people to learn and educate against the view that some people and some kinds of knowledge are worth more than others, but the other side of risk is hope and desire. To hope is to revitalise the present by undermining the sense that the way things are currently is inevitable and immutable (Halpin, 2003). To foster desire means presenting alternative visions of what the future could be. Engaging with others in mutual learning is both a source for and potential outcome of hope and hope is closely bound up with the willingness to experiment, to make choices, to be adventurous. So hope and desire have creative roles in encouraging the development of imaginative and transgressive solutions to seemingly intractable difficulties. For community educators this vision is about fostering a desire to know more, and a belief, however tenuous, in the possibility of doing so. It is about education that moves away from inequitable, individualised, deficit models of learning and brings about change in understanding both self and society that leads on to a more equitable life for everyone. Having such a vision before us helps us to take those steps that in the end make a broad path as we walk towards a more democratically just society.

References

Adam, B., Beck, U. and Van Loon, J. (2000) *The Risk Society and Beyond: Critical Issues for Social Theory*, London: Sage

Advisory Group on Citizenship (1998) *Education for Citizenship and the Teaching of Democracy in Schools*, London: Qualifications and Curriculum Authority

Aldridge, F. and Tuckett, A. (2008) *Counting the Cost*, Leicester: National Institute of Adult Continuing Education

Alexander, D., Leach, T. and Steward, T. (1984) 'Adult education in the context of community education: progress and regress in the Tayside, Central and Fife regions of Scotland in the nine years since the Alexander Report', *Studies in the Education of Adults*, Vol. 16, pp. 39–57

Alexander, K. (1993) 'Critical reflections', *Edinburgh Review*, Vol. 90, pp. 29–40

Apple, M. W. (2006) *Educating the 'Right' Way: Markets, Standards, God and Inequality* (second edn), New York: Routledge

Arshad, R. (1999) 'Making racism visible: an agenda for an anti-racist Scotland', in Crowther *et al.* (eds) (1999), pp. 279–89

Ball, S. J. (1990) *Politics and Policy-Making in Education*, London: Routledge

Barnes, C., Mercer, G. and Shakespeare, T. (1999) *Exploring Disability: A Sociological Introduction*, Cambridge: Polity Press

Barnett, S. (1898) 'Review of the possibilities of settlement life', in Reason, W. (ed.) (1898) *University and Social Settlements*, London: Methuen, pp. 10–19

Barr, J. (1999) 'Women, adult education and really useful knowledge', in Crowther *et al.* (eds) (1999), pp. 70–82

Barry, M. (ed.) (2005) *Youth Policy and Social Inclusion: Critical Debates with Young People*, Abingdon: Routledge

Batsleer, J. R. (2008) *Informal Learning in Youth Work*, London: Sage

Beresford, P. and Croft, S. (1993) *Citizen Involvement, a Practical Guide for Change*, London: Macmillan

Biesta, G. (2006) 'What's the point of lifelong learning if lifelong learning has no point? On the democratic deficit of policies for lifelong learning', *European Educational Research Journal*, Vol. 5, Nos 3 and 4, pp. 169–80

Biesta, G. (2009) 'Good education in an age of measurement: on the need to reconnect with the question of purpose in education', *Educational Assessment, Evaluation and Accountability*, Vol. 21, pp. 33–46

Blair, A. (1998) quoted in Department for Education and Employment, *The Learning Age: A Renaissance for a New Britain*, London: DfEE, Cm3790, p. 9

Blanch, M. (1979) 'Imperialism, nationalism and organized youth', in Clarke, J. *et. al.* (eds) (1979) *Working Class Culture*, London: Hutcheson, pp. 52–61

Brine, J. (2006) 'Lifelong learning and the knowledge economy – those that know and those that do not – the discourse of the European Union', *British Educational Research Journal*, Vol. 32,

No. 5, pp. 649–65

Bowe, R. and Ball, S. with Gold, A. (1992) *Reforming Education and Changing Schools*, London: Routledge and Kegan Paul

Brent, J. (2004) 'The desire for community: illusion, confusion, paradox', *Community Development Journal*, Vol. 39, No. 3, pp. 213–23

Brookfield, S. (2000) 'Adult cognition as a dimension of lifelong learning', in Field, and Leicester (eds) (2000), pp. 89–101

Bryant, I. (1984) *Radicals and Respectables: The Adult Education Experience in Scotland*, Edinburgh: Scottish Institute of Adult Education

Burke, B. (2009) 'Chartism, education and community', in Gilchrist, R., Jeffs, T., Spence, J. and Walker, J. (eds) (2009) *Essays in the History of Youth and Community Work*, Lyme Regis: Russell House Publishing, pp. 56–68

Carlisle, S. (2001) 'Inequalities in health: contested explanations, shifting discourses and ambiguous policies', *Critical Public Health*, Vol. 11, No. 3, pp. 89–91

Carnoy, M. and Levin, H. (1985) *Schooling and Work in the Democratic State*, Stanford: Stanford University Press

Coffield, F. (1999) 'Breaking the consensus: lifelong learning as social control', *British Educational Research Journal*, Vol. 25, No. 4, pp. 479–99

Cohen, A. P. (1985) *The Symbolic Construction of Community*, London: Tavistock

Cole, G. D. H. (1930) *The Life of Robert Owen*, revised edn, London: Macmillan

Coleman, S. and Rowe, C. (2005) *Remixing Citizenship: Democracy and Young People's Use of the Internet*, London: Carnegie Young People Initiative

Coles, B. (1995) *Youth and Social Policy: Youth Citizenship and Young Careers*, London: UCL Press

Commission of the European Communities (CEC) (1993) *Background Report: Social Exclusion, Poverty and Other Social Problems in the European Community*, Brussels: Directorate General for Education, Training and Youth

Commission of the European Communities (1994) *Growth, Competitiveness, Employment: The Challenges and Way Forward into the 21st Century*, Brussels: Directorate General for Education, Training and Youth

Commission of the European Communities (1995) *Teaching and Learning – Towards the Learning Society*, Brussels: Directorate General for Education, Training and Youth

Commission of the European Communities (1998) *Learning for Active Citizenship*, Brussels: Directorate General for Education, Training and Youth

Commission of the European Communities (CEC) (2000) *A Memorandum on Lifelong Learning*, Brussels: Directorate General for Education, Training and Youth

Commission of the European Communities (2004) *Progress towards the Common Objectives in Education and Training: Indicators and Benchmarks*, Brussels: Commission Staff Working Paper, SEC 73

Commission of the European Communities (2005) *Progress towards the Lisbon Objectives in Education and Training*, Brussels: Commission Staff Working Paper, SEC 419

Commission of the European Communities (2006) *Adult Learning: It is Never Too Late to Learn*, Brussels: Directorate General for Education, Training and Youth

Communities Scotland (2005) *National Standards for Community Engagement*, Edinburgh: Communities Scotland/Scottish Executive

Communities Scotland and Scottish Executive (2004) *Working and Learning Together to Build Stronger Communities* ('WALT'), Edinburgh: Scottish Executive

Communities Scotland and Scottish Executive (2005) *An Adult Literacy and Numeracy Curriculum for Scotland*, Edinburgh: Scottish Executive

Communities Scotland and Scottish Executive (2007) *Delivering Change: Understanding the*

Outcomes of Community Learning and Development, Edinburgh: Communities Scotland

Confederation of Scottish Local Authorities (1995) *Community Education: Its Place in Local Government*, Edinburgh: COSLA

Confederation of Scottish Local Authorities (1998) *Promoting Learning – Developing Opportunities: A COSLA Consultation Paper on the Future Development of Local Authority Community Education in Scotland*, Edinburgh: COSLA

Confederation of Scottish Local Authorities and Scottish Government (2008) *Building on 'Working and Learning Together to Build Stronger Communities': The Role of Community Learning and Development (CLD) in Delivering Change*, Edinburgh: Scottish Government

Considine, M. (2005) *Making Public Policy: Institutions, Actors, Strategies*, Cambridge: Polity Press

Cooke, A. (2006) *From Popular Education to Lifelong Learning: A History of Adult Education in Scotland 1707–2005*, Leicester: National Institute of Adult Continuing Education

Cornwall, A. (2008) 'Unpacking "participation": models, meanings and practices', *Community Development Journal*, Vol. 43, No. 3, pp. 269–83

Craig, G., Derricourt, N. and Loney, M. (eds) (1982) *Community Work and the State*, London: Routledge and Kegan Paul

Craig, G., Taylor, M., Wilkinson, M. and Monro, S. with Bloor, K. and Syed, A. (2002) *Contract or Trust? The Role of Compacts in Local Governance*, Bristol: Policy Press and York: Joseph Rowntree Foundation

Crossley, N. (2004) 'Not being mentally ill: social movements, system survivors and the oppositional habitus', *Anthropology and Medicine*, Vol. 11, No. 2, pp. 161–80

Crowther, J. (1999) 'Popular education and the struggle for democracy', in Crowther *et al.* (eds) (1999), pp. 29–40

Crowther, J. (2006) 'Social movements, praxis and the profane side of lifelong learning', in Sutherland, P. and J. Crowther, J. (eds) (2006) *Lifelong Learning*, London: Routledge, pp. 171–81

Crowther J. and Martin, I. (2006) 'Adult education in Scotland: retrospect and prospect', *Papers d'Educacio de Persones Adultes*, Vols 51–2, pp. 21–3

Crowther, J., Martin, I. and Shaw, M. (eds) (1999) *Popular Education and Social Movements in Scotland Today*, Leicester: National Institute of Adult Continuing Education

Crowther, J. and Tett, L. (2001) 'Democracy as a way of life: literacy for citizenship', in Crowther, J., Hamilton, M. and Tett, L. (eds) (2001) *Powerful Literacies*, Leicester: National Institute of Adult Continuing Education, pp. 108–18

Cullen, J. (2001) 'Re-shaping identity: the wider benefits of learning', in Coffield, F. (ed.) (2001) *What Progress are We Making with Lifelong Learning? The Evidence from Research*, Newcastle upon Tyne: Department of Education, University of Newcastle, pp. 63–76

Darmon, I., Frade, C. and Hadjivassilliou, K. (1999) 'The comparative dimension in continuous vocational training: a preliminary framework', in Coffield, F. (ed.) (1999) *Why's the Beer Up North Always Stronger? Studies of Lifelong Learning in Europe*, Bristol: Policy Press, pp. 31–42

Davie, G. (1961) *The Democratic Intellect: Scotland and her Universities in the Nineteenth Century*, Edinburgh: Edinburgh University Press

Department for Education and Employment (1995) *Lifetime Learning – A Consultation Document*, Sheffield: DfEE

Department for Education and Employment (1998) *The Learning Age: A Renaissance for a New Britain*, London: DfEE

Department for Education and Skills (2005) *Skills: Getting on in Business, Getting on at Work*, London: DfES

Donnachie, I. (2003) 'Education in Robert Owen's new society: the New Lanark Institute and schools', *The Encyclopaedia of Informal Education* (online). Available from URL: www.infed.

org/thinkers/et-owen.htm (accessed 10 April 2010)

Dwyer, P. and Wyn, J. (2001) *Youth, Education and Risk: Facing the Future*, London: Routledge Falmer

Eccelstone, K. (2004) 'Learning or therapy? The demoralization of education, *British Journal of Educational Studies*, Vol. 52, No. 2, pp. 112–37

Etzioni, A. (1993) *The Spirit of Community: The Reinvention of Modern American Society*, New York: Simon and Schuster

Fauré, E., Herrera, F., Kaddoura, A. *et al.* (1972) *Learning to Be: The World of Education Today and Tomorrow*, Paris: UNESCO

Field, J. (2000) *Lifelong Learning and the New Educational Order*, Stoke on Trent: Trentham Books

Field, J. and Leicester, M. (eds) (2000) *Lifelong Learning: Education across the Lifespan*, London: Routledge

Fisher, D. (1999) '"A band of little comrades": Socialist Sunday Schools in Scotland', in Crowther *et al.* (eds) (1999), pp. 136–42

Fraser, N. (1997) 'From redistribution to recognition? Dilemmas of justice in a "postsocialist" age', in Fraser, N. (1997) *Justice Interruptus*, New York: Routledge, pp. 1–26

Freire, P. (1972) *Pedagogy of the Oppressed*, Harmondsworth: Penguin

Fryer, R. H. (1997) *Learning for the Twenty First-Century*, London: DfEE

Furedi, F (1997) *A Culture of Fear: Risk-Taking and the Morality of Low Expectations*, London: Cassell

Furlong A. and Cartmel, F. (2007) *Young People and Social Change: Individualisation and Risk in Later Modernity*, second edn, Buckingham: Open University Press

Fyfe, I. (2003) 'Young Scots', in Crowther, J., Martin, I. and Shaw, M. (eds) (2003) *Renewing Democracy in Scotland: An Educational Source Book*, Leicester: National Institute of Adult Continuing Education, pp. 113–16

Gattrell, A. Thomas, C., Bennett, S., Bostock, L., Popay, J., Williams, G. and Shahtahmasebi, S. (2000) 'Understanding health inequalities: locating people in geographical and social spaces', in Graham, H. (ed.) (2000) *Understanding Health Inequalities*, Buckingham: Open University Press, pp. 41–59

Graham, H. (ed.) (2000) *Understanding Health Inequalities*, Buckingham: Open University Press

Griffin, C. (2004) 'Representations of the young', in Roche, J. and Tucker, S. (eds) (2004) *Youth in Society: Contemporary Theory, Policy and Practice*, second edn, London: Sage, pp. 10–18

Habermas, J. (1989) *The Theory of Communicative Action*, Vol 2 translated by Thomas McCarthy, Cambridge: Polity Press

Hall, T., and Williamson, H. (1999) 'Learning for citizenship', *UK Youth*, winter, pp. 12–14

Hall, T., Williamson, H. and Coffey, A. (2000) 'Young people, citizenship and the third way: a role for the Youth Service?' *Journal of Youth Studies*, Vol. 3, No. 4, pp. 461–72

Hammond, C. (2004) 'Impacts on well-being mental health and coping', in Schuller T., Brasset-Grundy, A., Green, A., Hammond, C. and Preston, J. (2004) *Wider Benefits of Learning*, London: RoutledgeFalmer, pp. 37–56

Halpin, D. (2003) *Hope and Education*, London: RoutledgeFalmer

Harvey, D. (1989) *The Urban Experience,* Oxford: Blackwell

Hatcher, R. and Leblond, D. (2001) 'Education Action Zones and Zones d'Education Prioritaires' in Riddell, S. and Tett, L. (eds) (2001) *Education, Social Justice and Inter-Agency Working: Joined Up or Fractured Policy?* London: Routledge, pp. 29–57

Heath, S. B. (1983) *Ways with Words: Language, Life and Work in Communities and Classrooms*, Cambridge: Cambridge University Press

Helve, H. (1997) 'Perspectives on social exclusion, citizenship and youth', in Bynner, J., Chisholm, L. and Furlong, A. (eds) (1997) *Youth Citizenship and Social Change in a European Context*,

Aldershot: Ashgate, pp. 228–33

Hendry, L., Craik, I. Love, J. and Mack, J. (1991) *Measuring the Benefits of Youth Work*, Edinburgh: Scottish Office Education Department

Her Majesty's Inspectorate of Education (HMIE) (2003) *Citizenship in Youth Work*, Edinburgh: HMIE

HM Treasury (1999) *Tackling Poverty and Extending Opportunity*, London: HMSO

Hine, J. and Wood, J. (2009) 'Working with young people: emergent themes', in Wood, J. and Hine, J. (eds) (2009) *Work with Young People: Theory and Policy for Practice*, London: Sage, pp. 247–55

Holford, J., Riddell, S., Weedon, E., Litjens, J. and Hannan, G. (2008) *Patterns of Lifelong Learning: Policy and Practice in an Expanding Europe*, Wien: Lit Verlag

Holyoake, G. J. (1896) *Sixty Years of an Agitator's Life*, third edn, London: Fisher Unwin

Hudson, J. (2006) 'Inequality and the knowledge economy: running to stand still'? *Social Policy and Society*, Vol. 5, No. 2, pp. 207–22

Jackson, K. (1995) 'Popular education and the state: a new look at the community debate', in Mayo, M. and Thompson, J. (eds) (1995) *Adult Learning, Critical Intelligence and Social Change*, Leicester: National Institute of Adult Continuing Education, pp. 182–203

Jeffs, T. (1997) 'Changing their ways: youth work and the "underclass" theory', in MacDonald, R. (ed.) (1997) *Youth, the 'Underclass' and Social Exclusion*, Routledge, London, pp. 153–66

Jeffs, T. (1998) 'Wild things? Young people, our new "enemy within"', *Concept*, Vol. 8, No. 1, 1998, pp. 8–11

Jeffs, T. (2004) 'Curriculum debate: a letter to Jon Ord', *Youth and Policy*, No. 84, summer, pp. 55–61

Jeffs, T. and Smith, M. K. (eds) (1990) *Using Informal Education*, Milton Keynes: Open University Press

Johnson, R. (1988) 'Really useful knowledge, 1790–1850', in Lovett, T. (ed.) (1988) *Radical Approaches to Adult Education: A Reader*, London: Routledge, pp. 3–34

Johnston, R. (2000) 'Community education and lifelong learning: local spice for global fare,' in Field and Leicester (eds) (2000), pp. 12–28

Jones, D. (1981) 'Community work in the United Kingdom', in Henderson, P. and Thomas, D. N. (eds) (1981) *Readings in Community Work*, London: Allen and Unwin, pp. 121–31

Jones, G. and Wallace, C. (1992) *Youth, Family and Citizenship*, Milton Keynes: Open University Press

Jones, J. (1999a) *Private Troubles and Public Issues, a Community Development Approach to Health*, Edinburgh: Community Learning Scotland

Jones, J. (1999b) *Writing about Health Issues: Voices from Communities*, Edinburgh: Moray House Institute of Education

Jones, J. (2001) *Writing about Health Issues: Voices from Communities Volume 2*, Edinburgh: Moray House Institute of Education

Jonker, E. (2006) 'School hurts: refrains of hurt and hopelessness in stories about dropping out at a vocational school of care work', *Journal of Education and Work*, Vol. 19, No. 2, pp. 121–40

Kirkwood, C. (1990) *Vulgar Eloquence: Essays in Education, Community and Politics*, Edinburgh: Polygon

Kovacheva, S. (2005) 'Will youth rejuvenate the patterns of political participation?', in Forbig, J. (ed.) (2005) *Revisiting Youth Political Participation: Challenge for Research and Democratic Practice in Europe*, Strasbourg: Council of Europe, pp. 19–28

Labonte, R. (1997) 'Community, community development and the forming of authentic partnerships', in Minkler, M. (ed.) (1997) *Community Organising and Community Building for Health*, New Brunswick: Rutgers University Press, pp. 18–27

Lawson, H. (2001) 'Active citizenship in schools and the community', *The Curriculum Journal*, No. 12, pp. 163–78

Learning and Teaching Scotland (2002) *Education for Citizenship in Scotland: A Paper for Discussion and Development*, Dundee: LTS

Leat, D. (1975) 'Social theory and the historical construction of social work activity: the role of Samuel Barnett', in Leonard, P. (ed.) (1975) *The Sociology of Community Action*, Stafford: University of Keele, pp. 25–34

Levin, H. M. and Kelley, C. (1997) 'Can education do it alone?', in Halsey, A. H., Lauder, H., Brown, P. and Wells, A. S. (eds) (1997) *Education: Culture, Economy and Society*, Oxford: Oxford University Press, pp. 25-32

Lisbon European Council (2000) *Presidency conclusions* (online). Available from URL: www.con-silium.europa.eu/ueDocs/cms_Data/.../00100-r1.en0.htm (accessed 10 April 2010)

Lister, R. (1997) 'Citizenship: towards a feminist synthesis', *Feminist Review*, 57, autumn, pp. 28–48

Luttrell, W. (1997) *School-Smart and Mother-Wise*, London: Routledge

MacDonald, R. (ed.) (1997) *Youth, the 'Underclass' and Social Exclusion*, London: Routledge

Macintyre, S. (2007) *Inequalities in Health in Scotland: What Are They and What Can We Do about Them?* Glasgow: MRC Social and Public Health Sciences Unit

Maclachlan, K. and Tett, L. (2006) 'Learning to change or changing the learning: adult literacy and numeracy in Scotland', *Journal of Adult and Continuing Education*, Vol. 12, No. 2, pp. 195–206

Malone, K. (2002) 'Street life: youth, culture and competing uses of public space', *Environment and Urbanization*, Vol. 14, No. 2, pp. 157–68

Marmot, M. G. and Wilkinson, R. G. (2006) *Social Determinants of Health*, second edn, Oxford: Oxford University Press

Martin, I. (1987) 'Community education: towards a theoretical analysis', in Allen, G. and Martin, I. (eds) (1987) *Community Education: An Agenda for Educational Reform*, Milton Keynes: Open University Press, pp. 9–32

Martin, I. (1996) 'Community education: the dialectics of development', in Fieldhouse, R. *et al.* (1986) *A History of Modern British Adult Education*, Leicester: National Institute of Adult Continuing Education, pp. 109–41

Martin, I. (1999) 'Introductory essay: popular education and social movements in Scotland today', in Crowther *et al.* (eds) (1999), pp. 1–25

Martin, I. (2001) 'What is lifelong learning for: earning, yearning or yawning?', *Adults Learning*, Vol. 13, No. 2, pp. 14–17

Martin, I. (2003) 'Inflections of "community" in educational work and research', in Centre for Research into Lifelong Learning (2003) *Experiential Community: Work-based: Researching Learning Outside the Academy*, Glasgow: CRLL, pp. 270-6

Matthews, H. (2001) 'Citizenship, youth councils and young people's participation', *Journal of Youth Studies*, Vol. 4, No. 3, pp. 299–318

Mayo, M. (1975) 'Community development: a radical alternative?', in Bailey, R. and Brake, M. (eds) (1975) *Radical Social Work*, London: Edward Arnold, pp. 83–91

Mayo, M. (1997) 'Partnerships for regeneration and community development', *Critical Social Policy*, Vol. 52, pp. 3–26

McConnell, C. (ed.) (1996) *Community Education: The Making of an Empowering Profession*, Edinburgh: Scottish Community Education Council

Merton, B. and Wylie, T. (2004) 'The youth work curriculum: a response to Jon Ord', *Youth and Policy*, No. 85, summer, pp. 63–7

Milburn, T. (1999) 'Community education', in Bryce, T. G .K. and Hume, W. (eds) (1999) *Scottish Education*, Edinburgh: Scottish Academic Press, pp. 837–46

Miliband, R. (1994) *Socialism for a Sceptical Age*, London: Polity Press

Mills, C. W. (1959) *The Sociological Imagination*, London: Oxford University Press

Mohanty, C. (1994) 'On race and voice: challenges for liberal education in the 1990s, in Giroux, H. and McLaren, P. (eds) (1994) *Between Borders: Pedagogy and the Politics of Cultural Studies*, London: Routledge, pp. 145–66

Montagu, L. H. (1904) 'The girl in the background', in Urwick, E. J. (1904) *Studies of Boy Life in Our Cities*, London: J. M. Dent, pp. 7–19

National Advisory Council for Education and Training Targets (1998) *Fast Forward for Skills*, London: NACETT

Newman, J., Glendinning, C. and Hughes, M. (2008) 'Beyond modernisation? Social care and the transformation of welfare governance', *Journal of Social Policy*, Vol. 37, No. 4, pp. 531–57

NHS Health Scotland (2009) *Health in Scotland, Report of the Chief Medical Officer* (online). Available from URL: www.scotland.gov.uk/Publications/2009/12/16103619/7 (accessed 10 April 2010)

Ord, J. (2007) *Youth Work Process, Product and Practice*, Lyme Regis: Russell House Publishing

Owen, D. (2006) 'The internet and youth civic engagement in the United States', in Oates, S., Owen, D. and Gibson, R. K. (eds) (2006) *The Internet and Politics: Citizens, Voters and Activists*, London: Routledge, pp. 20–38

Owen, R. (1816) *An Address to the Inhabitants of New Lanark*, London (online). Available from URL: www.infed.org/archives/e-texts/owen_new_lanark.htm (accessed 10 April 2010)

Payne, M. (2009) 'Modern youth work: purity or common cause?', in Wood and Hine (eds) (2009), pp. 213–32

Percy-Smith, B. (2006) 'From consultation to social learning in community participation with young people', *Children, Youth and Environments*, Vol. 16, No. 2, pp. 153–79

Perkins, D. F. (2009) 'Community youth development', in Wood and Hine (eds) (2009), pp. 104–13

Pimlott, J. A. R. (1935) *Toynbee Hall: Fifty Years of Social Progress 1884–1934*, London: Dent

Plant, R. (1974) *Community and Ideology: An Essay in Applied Social Philosophy*, London: Routledge and Kegan Paul

Pollard, S. (1963) 'Factory discipline in the industrial revolution', *Economic History Review*, Vol. 16, pp. 254–71

Purdue D., Razzaque, K., Hambleton, R., Stewart, M. with Huxham, C. and Vangen, S. (2000) *Community Leadership in Area Regeneration*, Bristol: Policy Press

Ranson S. (1994) *Towards the Learning Society*, London: Cassel Education

Ranson S. (1998) *Inside the Learning Society*, London: Cassel Education

Rape Crisis (2009) *This is not an invitation to rape me* (online). Available from URL: www.thisis-notaninvitationtorapeme.co.uk/ (accessed 10April 2010)

Reay, D., Crozier, G. and Clayton, J. (2010) '"Fitting in" or "standing out": working class students in higher education', *British Educational Research Journal*, Vol. 36, No. 1, pp. 107–24

Rees, G., Fevré, R., Furlong, A. and Gorard, S. (1997) *Notes towards a Social Theory of Lifetime Learning: History, Place and the Learning Society*, Cardiff: University of Cardiff, School of Education, Working Paper 6

Ritzer, G. (2000) *The McDonaldization of Society*, Thousand Oaks: Pine Forge Press

Rogoff, B. (2003) *The Cultural Nature of Human Development*, Oxford: Oxford University Press

Rose, M. (2001) 'The secular faith of the settlements', in Gilchrist, R. and Jeffs, T. (eds) (2001) *Settlements, Social Change and Community Action*, London: Jessica Kingsley, pp. 64–71

Russell, H. (2001) *Local Strategic Partnerships: Lessons from New Commitment to Regeneration*, Bristol: Policy Press/Joseph Rowntree Foundation

Russell, C. E. B. and Rigby, L. M. (1908) *Working Lads' Clubs*, London: Macmillan

Samoff, J. (1990) '"Modernizing" a socialist vision: education in Tanzania', in Carnoy, M. and Samoff, J. (eds) (1990) *Education and Social Transition in the Third World*, Princeton, NJ: Princeton University Press, pp. 82–93

Schon, D. (1983) *The Reflexive Practitioner: How Professionals Think in Action*, London: Temple Smith

Schuller, T. and Watson, D. (2009) *Learning through Life: Inquiry into the Future for Lifelong Learning*, Leicester, National Institute of Adult Continuing Education

Scott, G. (1998) *Feminism and the Politics of Working Women*, London: UCL Press

Scottish Community Education Council (1984) *Training for Change*, Edinburgh: SCEC

Scottish Community Education Council (1986) *Our Tomorrow. Policy Statement on Youth Work in Scotland*, Edinburgh: SCEC

Scottish Community Education Council (1989) *Community Development in the Community Education Service*, Edinburgh: SCEC

Scottish Community Education Council (1996) prepared by United Kingdom Youth Work Alliance, *Agenda for a Generation – Building Effective Youth Work*, Edinburgh: SCEC

Scottish Education Department (SED) (1975) *Adult Education: The Challenge of Change*, Edinburgh: HMSO

Scottish Education Department (1977) *Professional Education and Training for Community Education* (The Carnegie Report), Edinburgh: HMSO

Scottish Executive (1998a) *Opportunity Scotland: A Paper on Lifelong Learning*, Edinburgh: Scottish Executive

Scottish Executive (1998b) *Social Inclusion Strategy for Scotland*, Edinburgh: Scottish Executive

Scottish Executive (1999) *Skills for Scotland: A Skills Strategy for a Competitive Scotland*, Edinburgh: Scottish Executive

Scottish Executive (2000a) *Empowered to Practice*, Edinburgh: Stationary Office

Scottish Executive (2000b) *Scotland: The Learning Nation*, Edinburgh: Scottish Executive

Scottish Executive (2000c) *Social Justice Annual Report*, Edinburgh: Scottish Executive

Scottish Executive (2000d) *Making It Happen. Report of the Strategy Action Team* (online). Available from URL: www.scotland.gov.uk/inclusion/docs/maih-03.htm (accessed 10 April 2010)

Scottish Executive (2001) *Adult Literacy and Numeracy in Scotland*, Edinburgh: Scottish Executive

Scottish Executive (2002) *Better Communities in Scotland: Closing the Gap*, Edinburgh: Scottish Executive

Scottish Executive (2003a) *Life Through Leaning; Learning Through Life, summary*, Edinburgh: Scottish Executive

Scottish Executive, (2003b) *Empowered to Practice: The Future of Community Development Training in Scotland*, Edinburgh: Scottish Executive

Scottish Executive (2004) *Curriculum for Excellence*, Edinburgh: Scottish Executive

Scottish Executive (2005a) *Measurement of the Extent of Youth Crime in Scotland*, Edinburgh: Scottish Executive in association with DTZ Pieda Consulting and National Centre for Social Research

Scottish Executive (2005b) *Public Attitudes to Participation,* Edinburgh: Scottish Executive

Scottish Executive (2006) *Strengthening Standards: Improving the Quality of Community Learning and Development Service Delivery*, Edinburgh: Scottish Executive

Scottish Government (2007a) *Scottish Budget Spending Review 2007*, Edinburgh: The Scottish Government

Scottish Government (2007b) *Skills for Scotland: A Lifelong Skills Strategy*, Edinburgh: Scottish Government

Scottish Government (2008a) *Up-Skilling the Community Learning and Development (CLD) Workforce: Position Statement*, Edinburgh: Learning Connections: Lifelong Learning

Directorate Scottish Government

Scottish Government (2008b) *Evaluation of the Impact of the National Standards for Community Engagement*, Glasgow: Housing and Regeneration, Scottish Government

Scottish Government (2008c) *The United Nations Convention of the Rights of the Child Explained*, Edinburgh: Scottish Government

Scottish Government (2008d) *Attitudes towards Youth Crime, and Willingness to Intervene: Findings from the 2006 Scottish Social Attitudes Survey*, Edinburgh: Scottish Government

Scottish Government (2009) *Community: Scottish Community Empowerment Action Plan*, Edinburgh: Scottish Government

Scottish Office (1998a) *Communities: Change Through Learning*, Edinburgh: Scottish Executive

Scottish Office (1998b) 'Changing the face of community education', press release, 17 November

Scottish Office Education and Industry Department (SOEID) (1997) *Lifelong Learning: The Way Forward*, Edinburgh: Scottish Office

Scottish Office Education and Industry Department (1999) *Circular 4/99: Community Education*, Edinburgh: HMSO

Select Committee on Education and Employment (1999) *Eighth Report: Access for All? A Survey of Post-16 Participation*, London: House of Commons (online). Available from URL: www.publications.parliament.uk/pa/cm199899/cmselect/cmeduemp/57 (accessed 10 April 2010)

Shakespeare, T. (1993) 'Disabled people's self-organisation: a new social movement?' *Disability, Handicap andw Society*, Vol. 8, No. 3, pp. 249–64

Shaw, Mae (2003) *Community Work: Policy, Politics and Practice*, Hull: Universities of Hull and Edinburgh

Shaw, Mae (2008) 'Community development and the politics of community', *Community Development Journal*, Vol. 43, No. 1, pp. 24–36

Silver, H. (1965) *The Concept of Popular Education*, London: MacGibbon and Kee

Smith, M. K. (1988) *Developing Youth Work*, Milton Keynes: Open University Press

Smith, M. K. (2007) 'Richard Henry Tawney, fellowship and adult education', *The Encyclopaedia of Informal Education* (online). Available from URL: www.infed.org/thinkers/tawney.htm (accessed 10 April 2010)

Spence, J. (1999) 'Lily Montagu, girl's work and youth work', *The Encyclopaedia of Informal Education* (online). Available from URL: www.infed.org/thinkers/et-monta.htm (accessed 10 April 2010)

St Croix, T. (2009) 'Forgotten corners: a reflection on radical youth work in Britain', in Gilchrist, R., Jeffs, T., Spence, J. and Walker, J. (eds) (2009) *Essays in the History of Youth and Community Work*, Lyme Regis: Russell House Publishing, pp. 302–15

Standards Council for CLD (2009a) Home page of the Standards Council for Community Learning and Development for Scotland (online). Available from URL: www.cldstandardscouncil.org.uk/cld/ (accessed 10 April 2010)

Standards Council for CLD (2009b) *The Competences for Community Learning and Development* (online). Available from URL: www.cldstandardscouncil.org.uk/cld/202.html (accessed 10 April 2010)

Stanley, M. (1890) *Clubs for Working Girls*, London: Macmillan

Stanton, N. (2004) 'The youth work curriculum and the abandonment of informal education', *Youth and Policy*, No. 85, autumn, pp. 71–85

Storrie, T. (2004) 'Citizens or What?', in Roche, J. and Tucker, S. (eds) (2004) *Youth in Society*, second edn, Milton Keynes: Open University Press, pp. 52–60

Tawney, R. H. (1926) 'Adult education in the history of the nation', paper read at the Fifth Annual conference of the British Institute of Adult Education

Taylor, D. and Dorsey-Gaines, C. (1988) *Growing up Literate: Learning from Inner-City Families*,

Portsmouth, NH: Heinemann

Tett, L. (2005) 'Partnerships, community groups and social inclusion', *Studies in Continuing Education*, Vol. 27, No. 1, pp. 1–15

Tett, L., Bamber, J., Edwards, V., Martin, I. and Shaw, M. (2007) *Developing Competence: Early and Mid-Career in Community Learning and Development*, Edinburgh: Scottish Government

Tett, L. and Ducklin, A. (1995) 'Further Education Colleges and educationally disadvantaged adults', *Scottish Educational Review*, Vol. 27, No. 2, pp. 154–64

Tett, L., Hamilton, M. and Hillier, Y. (2006) *Adult Literacy, Numeracy and Language: Policy Practice, Research*, London: Open University Press

Tett, L. and Maclachlan, K. (2007) 'Adult literacy and numeracy, social capital, learner identities and self–confidence', *Studies in the Education of Adults*, Vol. 39, No. 2, pp. 150–67

Thompson, E. P. (1976) *William Morris*, New York: Pantheon Books

Thompson, J. (2000) 'Life politics and popular learning', in Field and Leicester (eds) (2000), pp. 134–45

Thompson, J. (2001) *Re-Rooting Lifelong Learning*, Leicester: National Institute of Adult Continuing Education

Tisdall, E. K. M. and Davis, J. (2004) 'Making a difference? Bringing children's and young people's views into policy-making', *Children and Society*, Vol. 18, pp. 131–42

Tisdall, E.K.M., Davis, J.M. and Gallagher, M. (2008) 'Reflecting upon children and young people's participation in the UK', *International Journal of Children's Rights*, Special Issue No. 16, pp. 343–54

Tonnies, F. (1957) *Community and Society*, Loomis, C. (ed. and trans.), East Lancing, MI: Michigan State University Press. (Original work published as *Gemeinschaft und Gesellschaft*, 1887)

Tudor Hart J. (1971) 'The inverse care law', *Lancet* 1971; i: 405–12

Usher, R. and Edwards, R. (1998) 'Confessing all? A postmodern guide to the counselling and guidance of adult learners', in Edwards, R., Harrison, R. and Tait A. (eds) (1998) *Telling Tales: Perspectives on Guidance and Counselling in Learning*, London: Routledge, pp. 215–22

Van der Pas, N. (2001) Address by the European Commission, in *Adult Lifelong Learning in a Europe of Knowledge*, Conference Report, Sweden, pp. 11–18

Vygotsky, L. S. (1986) *Thought and Language*, A. Kozulin (ed. and trans.), Cambridge, MA: MIT Press

Wallace, C. (1992) 'Critical language awareness in the EFL classroom', in Fairclough, N. (ed.) (1992) *Critical Language Awareness*, Harlow: Longman, pp. 59–92

Wenger, E. (1998) *Communities of Practice: Learning, Meaning and Identity*, Cambridge: Cambridge University Press

West, A. (1996) 'Citizenship, Children and Young People', *Youth and Policy*, No. 55, winter, pp. 69–74

White, R. and Wyn, J. (2004) *Youth and Society: Exploring the Social Dynamics of Youth Experience*, South Melbourne: Oxford University Press

Williams, F. (1993) 'Women and community', in Bornat, J. *et al.* (eds) (1993) *Community Care: A Reader*, Milton Keynes: Open University Press, pp. 51–63

Williams, F. (1999) 'Good enough principles for welfare', *Journal of Social Policy*, Vol. 28, No. 4, pp. 667–87

Williams, R. (1976) *Keywords: A Vocabulary of Culture and Society*, London: Fontana

Williamson, H. (1997) 'Youth work and citizenship', in Bynner, J., Chisholm, L. and Furlong, A. (eds) (1997) *Youth Citizenship and Social Change in a European Context*, Ashgate, Aldershot, pp. 196–213

Wood, J. (2009) 'Education for effective citizenship', in Wood and Hine (eds) (2009), pp. 141–53

Wood, J. and Hine, J. (eds) (2009) *Work with Young People: Theory and Policy for Practice*. London: Sage

Wyn, J. and White, R. (1997) *Rethinking Youth*. London: Sage

Yeo E. and Yeo, S. (1988) 'On the uses of community', in Yeo, S. (ed.) (1988) *New Views of Cooperation*, London: Routledge, pp. 5–13

Index

Note: page numbers in *italics* denote figures or tables